ULTRAMODERN

LIZ O'BRIEN

ULTRAMODERN
SAMUEL MARX

ARCHITECT
DESIGNER
ART COLLECTOR

DESIGN: STAFFORD CLIFF
MANAGING EDITOR: JANE K. CREECH
EDITORS: TERRA CHALBERG AND ANNE HELLMAN WHITE
PRODUCTION: DOMINICK J. SANTISE, JR.

POINTED LEAF PRESS, LLC.

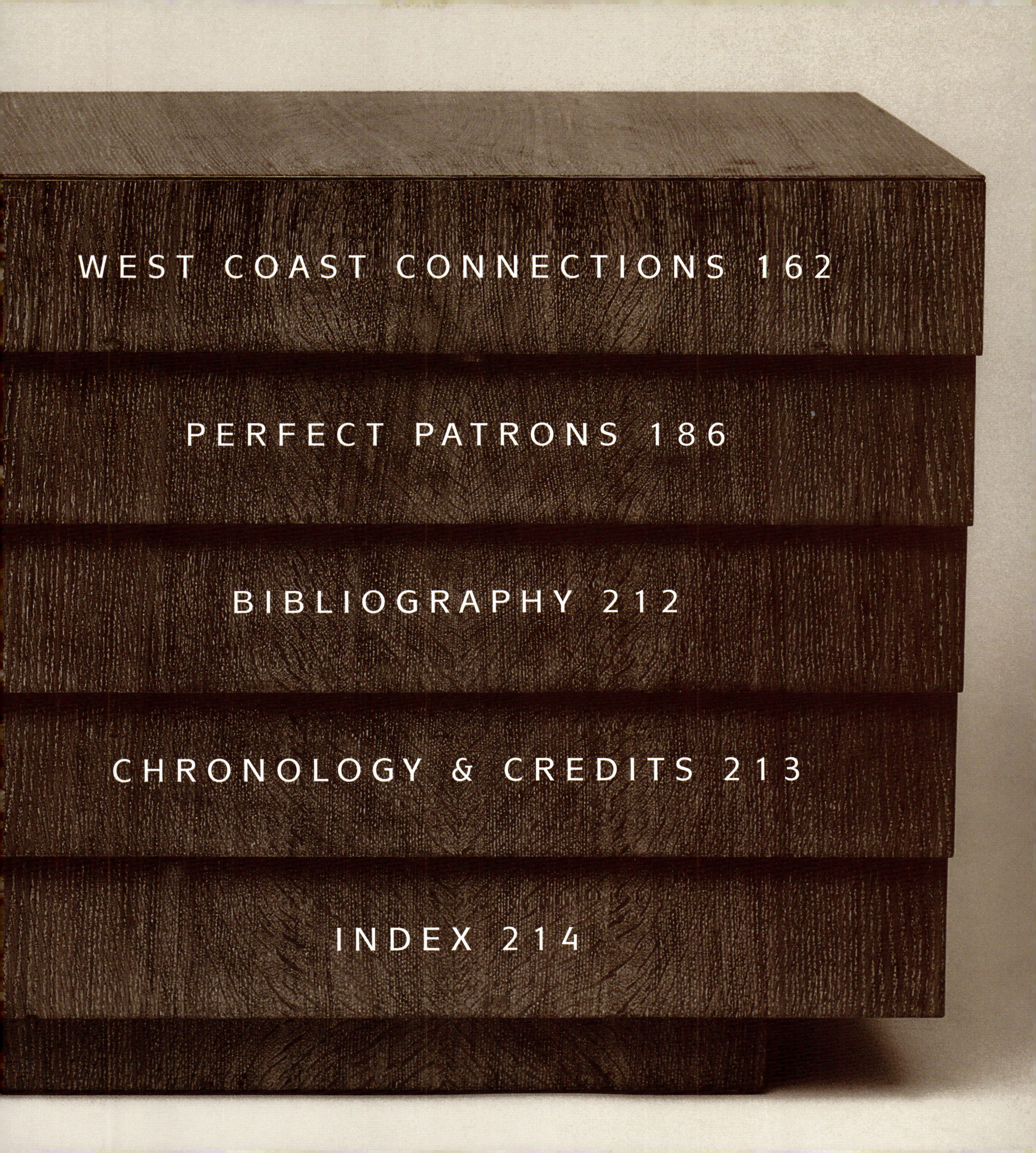

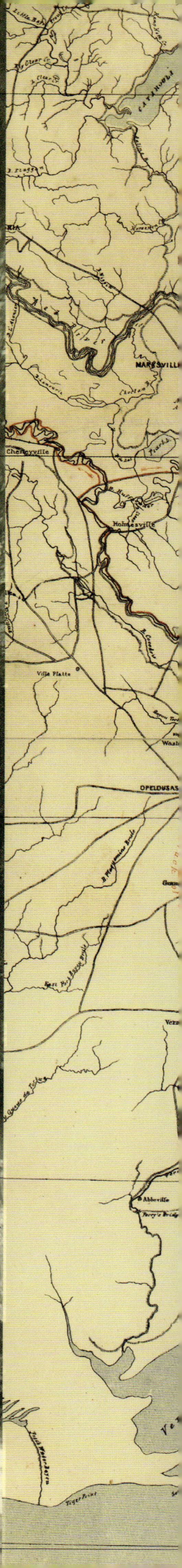
Cheneyville
Holmesville
Ville Platte
OPELOUSAS
Abbeville
Perry's Bridge

Period photographs belonging to Samuel Marx of antebellum houses in Natchez, Mississippi, include the portico of Auburn in Duncan Park, opposite, and the façade of Stanton Hall, above left. The Greek Revival door frame, above center, is at Jefferson College in Washington, Mississippi. Marx's parents settled in Natchez in the nineteenth century, and he was born there in 1885. The Southern town had a thriving industrial and merchant community, as shown in a street scene of around 1890, above right.

ABOVE The photograph of six-year-old Marx was taken in Monroe, Louisiana, about 100 miles from Natchez.
OPPOSITE In a family portrait of 1891, Marx was photographed with his parents, Annie, top left, and Jonas, top center.

ABOVE A view of the finely crafted flying staircase of Auburn, an 1812 mansion in Natchez, was in Marx's own collection of vintage photographs. OPPOSITE In 1930, the architect used a similar balustrade for a different type of spiral staircase at Edgecliff, Max Epstein's suburban Chicago estate.

OPPOSITE Marx, as he appeared in the 1907 yearbook of the Massachusetts Institute of Technology in Cambridge, Massachussetts, where he received his early training as an architect. He was twenty-one years old.

THIS PAGE Marx, photographed around 1950, was to have a successful architectural career in his adopted city of Chicago, Illinois.

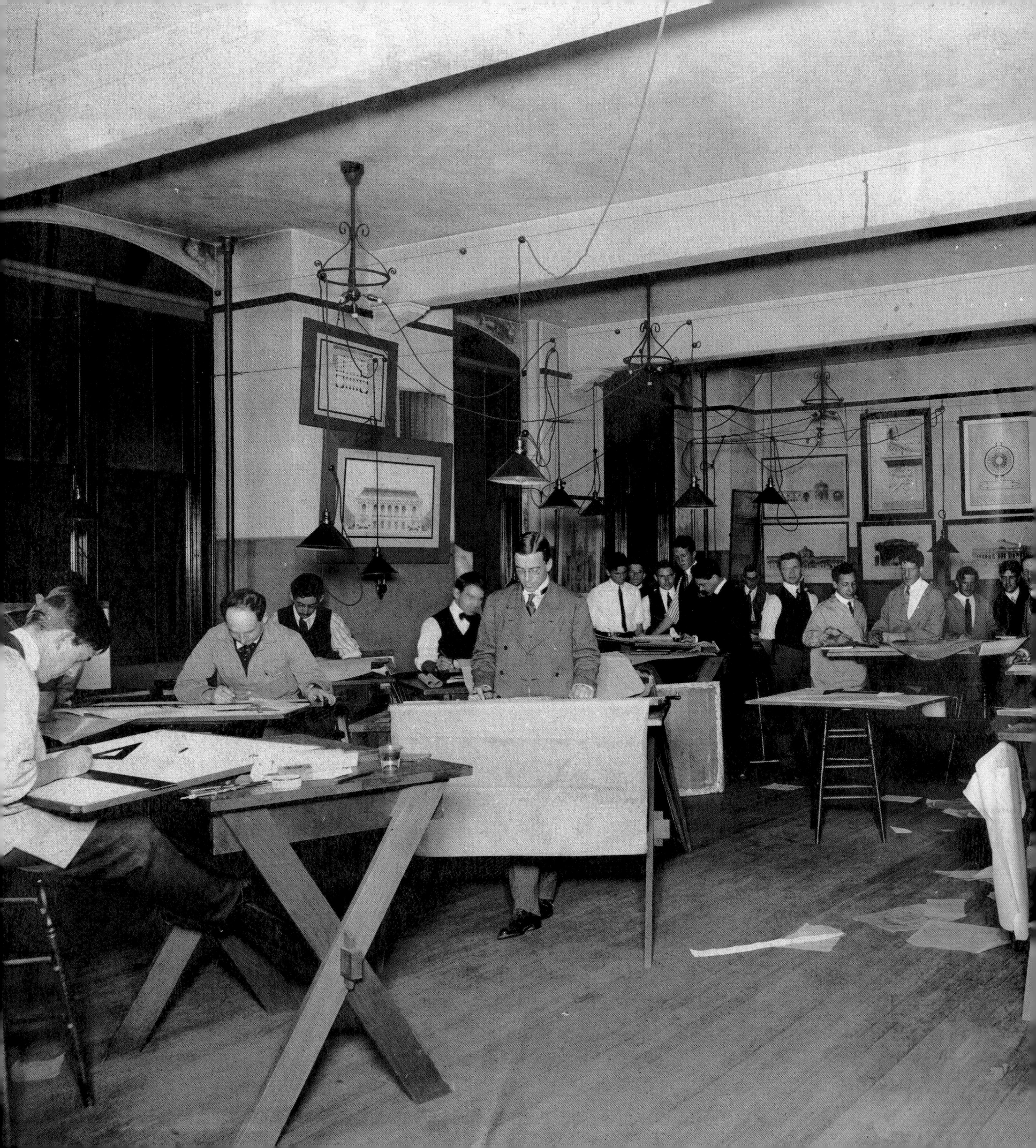

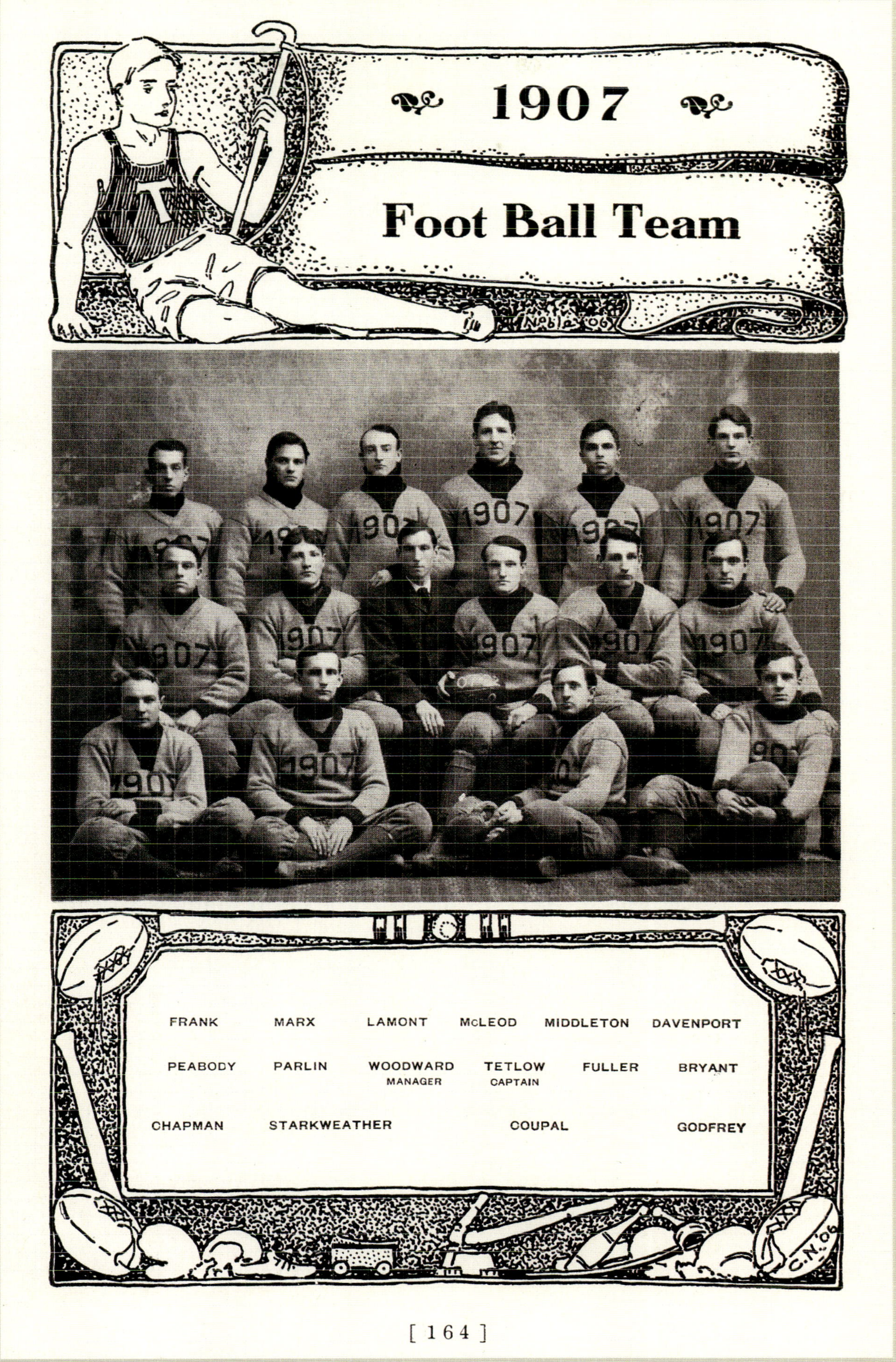

1907

Foot Ball Team

FRANK MARX LAMONT McLEOD MIDDLETON DAVENPORT

PEABODY PARLIN WOODWARD MANAGER TETLOW CAPTAIN FULLER BRYANT

CHAPMAN STARKWEATHER COUPAL GODFREY

[164]

OPPOSITE A scene from one of Désiré Despradelle's classes at the Massachusetts Institute of Technology, around 1898. The French-born Despradelle, whom Marx studied with, was known for his atelier-style method of teaching that was modeled on the same system as the Ecole des Beaux-Arts. ABOVE Marx (top row, second from left), as a member of the MIT football team of 1907.

ABOVE Marx designed a synagogue for his 1907 senior thesis at MIT. He was the only one in the class of twenty-two students to choose this subject. OPPOSITE His drafting skills are apparent in this rendering of the elevation of the domed stonework structure with its neoclassical and gothic details.

S B Thesis
Design for A Syna
Sam A. Ma

OPPOSITE The sculpture court at the Palais des études in Paris, with its glazed ceiling and arcaded galleries, showcased a host of classical figures. ABOVE The Cour d'Honneur at the Ecole des Beaux-Arts, where many American architects continued their classical training. Marx attended the school between 1907 and 1909.

BELOW Marx earned his first commission less than a year after his return to the United States, winning the competition to design the Isaac Delgado Museum of Art in New Orleans, Louisiana. Now known as the New Orleans Museum of Art, the building, which opened its doors in 1912, was, in Marx's own words "inspired by the Greek [but] sufficiently modified to give a subtropical appearance." Marx went on to cite the wice projection of the cornice to provide ample shade below, the open portico, and the tile roof, all informed by his southern upbringing.

RIGHT The Great Hall, or Statuary Hall, with its large, skylit open plan was designed for a collection of bronze and plaster casts of classical sculpture typical of museum collections at the time. The double staircase led to a gallery that wrapped around the second floor, providing exhibition space and also giving access to the upstairs exhibition rooms. The interior walls were sheathed in plaster colored and jointed to imitate Caen stone.

THESE PAGES Lake Shore Drive, in Chicago, hugs the Lake Michigan coastline, as seen in a photograph taken around 1916. ABOVE Marx lived for many years at 1325 North Astor Street, in this 1928 building in Chicago's Near North Side.

Samuel Abraham Marx was sui generis. Although he was one of many designers who worked in Chicago, Illinois, and helped make it the capital of American architecture in the first half of the twentieth century, he built a career and legacy unlike others of his generation. With a Beaux-Arts background and a modernist bent, Marx bridged classicism and modern styles to produce a body of work that was gracious, sophisticated, and timeless. When he took on a commission, he insisted on doing the interiors as well. The custom-made furniture pieces he designed for these projects have become prized touchstones of mid-century style.

When I opened a gallery in 1993 that specialized in French design of the 1940s, I knew very little about Samuel Marx. As the gallery grew, I started showing furniture by decorators such as William Haines and Dorothy Draper. One of the highlights of my job is doing research, and I often spend hours at the Cooper-Hewitt museum in New York and the New York Public Library. Appropriately, it was in the library's splendid Beaux-Arts reading room where I became intrigued with Marx's work. As I pored over back issues of *Architectural Forum* and *House & Garden*, I would find myself drawn over and over again to photographs of his commissions. I thought his serenely modern rooms were incomparable, and I longed to find examples of his furniture—a demilune table clad in parchment or a chest of drawers made to look like a stack of leather bound books—to exhibit at the gallery.

When I came across a cache of his work, it was everything I hoped it would be: luxurious, innovative, and beautifully crafted. There were cabinets in creamy crackle lacquer, parchment tables raised on Lucite slabs, a coffee table sheathed in squares of smoked mirror. Without knowing much about Marx's life or career, I knew that these works were exceptional and rare. Custom-made furniture by expert cabinetmakers is an anomaly of mid-century design. The era's most celebrated designers—Charles Eames, George Nelson, Isamu Noguchi—were creating mass-produced furniture for America's burgeoning postwar middle class, and subsequent scholarship has focused on these designs.

In those days—and it was not that long ago—books on modern design were few and far between, and Marx's work, which defied easy categorization, was hardly represented at all. I was eager to know more, and I began to do my own research, setting off on a treasure hunt that has taken me to Chicago, New Orleans, Los Angeles, and Natchez, Mississippi. One of my first stops was Bud Holland's gallery in Chicago, where Marx's furniture was shown amid a sophisticated mix of contemporary art, tribal works, and European decorative arts. Networking through friends, I learned about the photography archives at the Chicago Historical Society, and later, those of Julius Shulman in Los Angeles.

With Marx's credentials and numerous affiliations, I was sure I would come across an archive of office records, but I never did. When Marx closed his office in 1962, most of his papers were discarded. His conscientious and devoted secretary, Mary Temkin, returned blueprints, invoices, and correspondence to various clients. Some of these papers were later donated to the Art Institute of Chicago, and others were kept by relatives who shared them with me, but most are lost.

The challenges of researching Marx's life and career inspired me. In many cases the material had not been examined for many years, and I found myself literally blowing the dust off of old boxes. Photography archives became rich sources of information, providing names of clients and addresses in addition to visual records of Marx's work. Archivists, genealogists, family members, and his clients' heirs all helped assemble, mosaic-like, a picture of a unique figure among twentieth-century architects.

After Marx's first commission in 1910 for the Isaac Delgado Museum of Art in New Orleans, he went on to design a Pullman train car, swank supper clubs like the Pump Room in Chicago, and iconic department stores for the May Company. In residential work that ranged from country estates to modern houses to posh city apartments, Marx's skills as an architect were matched by his finely detailed interiors, reflecting his view that architecture and design should form a unified and harmonious whole. His furniture designs were made-to-order in Chicago by master cabinetmaker William J. Quigley. It was through this fruitful collaboration that Marx was able to realize his vision.

Samuel Abraham Marx was born to Jonas and Annie Marx in 1885 in Natchez. His German-born father, Jonas, had settled in the small Mississippi River city about 1880, joining relatives from his native Ingenheim. His mother, Annie Bazsinsky, who was born in New York in 1853, had roots in the pre–Civil War South; her father had been a successful cotton planter in nearby Warren County.

The Marx family was part of a small but vital community of Jewish immigrants who had settled in Natchez as early as 1840. A thriving commercial center in the nineteenth century, Natchez attracted tradesmen and merchants. By 1900 the B'nai Israel Congregation counted some 130 families as members. Jonas prospered as a merchant and by 1892 was joint proprietor of a wholesale liquor and tobacco business. As an only child (Marx's younger sister, who was born in 1887, died as an infant), Marx found company among friends and family in the tight-knit community of Natchez. His mother moved to Chicago in her old age and lived there until she died at 105. She always said that he was drawing as soon as he was old enough to hold a pencil.

When he was sixteen, his parents sent him north to the prestigious Phillips Exeter Academy in New Hampshire. After graduating from Exeter, he enrolled at the Massachusetts Institute of Technology in Cambridge, Massachusetts, where he received his Bachelor of Science in architecture in 1907. At MIT, Marx studied with Désiré Despradelle, a charismatic and influential French architect whose atelier style of teaching was modeled after the Ecole des Beaux-Arts in Paris, France. For his senior thesis, Marx produced a design for a domed synagogue with stained glass windows and classical and neo-Gothic details. Marx was no doubt inspired by the B'nai Israel temple in his hometown, which burned to the ground in 1903. A new building replaced it in 1905.

Like many American architects, including H. H. Richardson and Louis Sullivan, Marx continued his training in Paris at the Ecole des Beaux-Arts. Marx's contemporaries included David Adler, William Adams Delano, and Raymond Hood, all of whom went on to have distinguished careers that bridged traditional models with newly emerging modern styles. Seen from the vantage point of the twenty-first century, these links to the Beaux-Arts tradition reveal aspects of modernism that are just beginning to come into focus among scholars and collectors. Marx's work, which evolved over the early years of the twentieth century to culminate, at mid-century, in his own highly recognizable style, demonstrates the enduring value of classical standards and mirrors modern design's continuity with the past.

Marx's parents visited him both years he was at the Ecole des Beaux-Arts, which afforded him the opportunity to visit important architectural sites and cultural centers on the continent. The trips rounded out his education with an uncommon degree of exposure to cosmopolitan life and a firsthand knowledge of historic building styles.

The architecture of Marx's childhood also had a strong impact on his aesthetic. His own collection of vintage photographs of antebellum houses reveals the influence these Natchez sites had on his interest in architecture. Images of double-height porticos, Greek Revival doorways, and the exquisitely crafted freestanding staircase of Auburn, illustrate the sources that first sparked his young imagination. Marx would later draw on these forms, producing, most notably, his own version of the staircase for the Morton D. May house in 1941, rendering the modern model in smooth sculpted plaster.

Marx's first commission was in his native South. He won the 1910 competition to design the Isaac Delgado Museum of Art in New Orleans, beating out fifty-eight other entries. Now known as the New Orleans Museum of Art, it was, according to Marx, "inspired by the Greek [but] sufficiently modified to give a subtropical appearance." He noted that the wide projection of the cornice provided ample shade, which was necessary for the climate. The open portico and tile roof

OPPOSITE Marx was photographed at work in his office at 333 North Michigan Avenue in Chicago in the 1940s.

were no doubt informed by his Southern upbringing. Although the museum has expanded several times, Marx's original building remains largely intact.

When Marx moved to Chicago in 1910, the city was unquestionably the capital of American architecture; it was the home of skyscraper pioneer Daniel Burnham, who famously said, "Make no little plans; they have no magic to stir men's blood and probably will themselves not be realized." The city was on a long rebuilding boom necessitated by the Great Fire of 1871. After a brief stint as a draftsman at Shepley, Rutan and Coolidge, Marx went into business with Fred Lebenbaum, setting up the firm of Lebenbaum and Marx. Their early work, in addition to completing the museum, included a large country house in Glencoe, Illinois, completed in 1912 for Albert D. Lasker, the advertising tycoon. Lebenbaum died in 1916, and Marx eventually took on new associates, Noel L. Flint and Charles W. Schonne. The firm of Marx, Flint and Schonne had offices at 333 North Michigan Avenue, a prominent building designed by the firm of Holabird & Root.

Marx adapted quickly to life in Chicago, and became an active member of the city's well-to-do German-Jewish community. In 1916, he married Chicago native Margaret Schaffner, daughter of the head of the large men's clothing manufacturer Hart, Schaffner and Marx. By the 1920s, the couple was living in a house Marx designed for them at 1140 Sheridan Road in Glencoe, a short walk from the Lake Shore Country Club, the epicenter of Jewish social life on the North Shore. Nearly all of Marx's friends and clients—including the Bensingers, the Blocks, and the Rosenwalds—were part of this elite crowd. Most knew each other socially and, through business and family relations, club memberships and philanthropic organizations, shared many of the same civic and cultural affiliations.

Margaret and Sam later divorced, and after a brief period on his own, Marx married Lora Flanagan, an artist who had studied at Cranbrook Academy of Art under Swedish-born sculptor Carl Milles. This marriage ended in divorce in 1936. Lora Marx later became romantically involved with Mies van der Rohe, whom she met in 1940. While the two never married, they remained companions until Mies' death in 1969.

In the spring of 1937, Marx, then fifty-two, married Florene May Straus, the daughter of David May, who founded the May Company department store dynasty. Divorced with two children, Florene was seventeen years younger than Marx. The couple took an apartment at 1325 North Astor Street in Chicago's Gold Coast, where they lived for more than two decades, spending weekends at Marx's house in Glencoe. Together they would build a carefully edited modern art collection that made them formidable figures in the international art scene.

With Florene by his side, Marx became an impassioned collector. His deep appreciation for fine art had long informed his clients' purchases, and he fashioned his residential work around the sensitive installation of their paintings and sculpture. When the Marxes attended the 1939 Golden Gate Exposition in San Francisco, they made their first major purchase: George Braque's *Yellow Tablecloth* of 1935. For Marx, it was the beginning of a journey into a world that excited him as much as architecture and design, while engaging his intellect, curiosity, and visual acumen.

Upon returning to Chicago, Marx plunged headlong into seeking out top-notch works by the School of Paris artists he admired. He quickly acquired several important works by Henri Matisse, Pablo Picasso, and Constantin Brancusi. Many of these purchases were made through Pierre Matisse, the New York art dealer whose legendary gallery sponsored artists such as Alberto Giacometti and Joan Miró. Over the next twenty years, Marx and Matisse, a reticent man by nature, exchanged frequent correspondence that started out cordial and business-like, then slowly gained in warmth as their friendship grew. Matisse had great respect for the "quickness and sureness" of Marx's eye. Appreciative of Marx's commitment, Matisse often offered him first refusal when truly remarkable works became available.

Matisse was not, as one might have thought, the ipso facto representative of his father's work in the United States. Their complex relationship, chronicled by John Russell in his 1999 book *Father and Son*, was fraught with, among other things, the inevitable conflict between art and commerce. Pierre took pains not to confuse his filial role with the commercial demands of his gallery and hesitated to approach his father with advances of a business nature. Thus, it was Alfred H. Barr, Jr., of the Museum of Modern Art in New York, who helped Marx purchase two critical works by Matisse, *The Moroccans* (1915–16) and *Woman on a High Stool* (1914.) Marx purchased the former directly from the artist and the latter from his widow. The Marxes bought both paintings with the understanding that they would bequeath them to the Museum of Modern Art. When Marx finally succeeded in 1958 in acquiring *Woman on a High Stool*, which he had singled out years before, Pierre wrote to congratulate him: "I am glad you have the picture. I don't know anybody that could appreciate it more than you and Florene."

After World War II, the Marxes traveled abroad regularly, stopping in London and Paris and sometimes settling in Venice for long sojourns. On a trip to the South of France, the Marxes visited Picasso, who recommended three Paris dealers likely to have historic examples of his work. One of these was Heinz Berggruen, who admiringly recounts Marx's first visit to his gallery on the rue de l'Université in his memoir, *Highway and Byways*. Marx asked Berggruen to select the finest Picasso he had on hand with the understanding that he would be back the following day to see it. Berggruen produced, amazingly, the spectacular cubist painting *Woman with Pears* of 1909. Marx immediately recognized the work's outstanding quality and bought it straight away for the asking price.

The Marxes were known for their commitment to quality over quantity. As Berggruen's story indicates, the aim was to acquire only the very best, regardless of cost. James Thrall Soby, a curator, collector, and trustee of the Museum of Modern Art, wrote that the works had been "chosen with the rapt concentration of diamond cutters." Douglas Cooper, the well-known art historian and longtime friend of Picasso, included the Marxes in his 1963 book *Great Private Collections*, remarking on the Marxes "quiet exercise of impeccable taste."

The couple shared an interest not only in art but also in philanthropy. Marx, who had been active with the Art Institute of Chicago since 1917, served as a trustee from 1952 until the time of his death in 1964. Florene served on the Women's Board of the Art Institute. In 1953, Florene became a trustee of the Museum of Modern Art, and later a founding member of its International Council. The Marxes were well noted for their generosity, making numerous significant donations to both institutions as well as welcoming visitors to their home and graciously loaning works for exhibition.

By the late 1950s, the Marxes were no longer adding to the collection but remained deeply interested in the artists they admired. In 1960, in spite of Marx's failing health, the couple traveled to London to attend the historic Picasso retrospective at the Tate Gallery. They traveled with an entourage that included nurses and Marx's secretary. In 1962 the couple moved to New York and established residence at the Hotel Westbury. Marx's leaving was noted in the press, "An Era Ends, Sam Marx, Architect, Club Man, Bon Vivant Leaves Chicago," was the headline in one newspaper.

By this time, plans were already in the works for the exhibition of forty-four paintings from their collection for the School of Paris show at the Museum of Modern Art, which opened in 1965, one year after Marx's death. When Florene died in 1995, the collection was divided between the Museum of Modern Art and the Metropolitan Museum of Art to suit the needs of each institution.

Marx's own work is in the permanent collections of the Metropolitan Museum of Art, the Art Institute of Chicago, and the New Orleans Museum of Art. His timeless designs remain an eloquent expression of modernism's link to the past.

Liz O'Brien
May 2007, New York City

OPPOSITE In Glencoe, Illinois, a wood-paneled cabinet modeled on a Chinese scholar's study was designed by Marx in 1933 to house the fine jades that belonged to the Edward Sonnenscheins. The collection is now at the Art Institute of Chicago.

ABOVE Marx created the first aluminum train car for the Pullman Company, which was headquartered in Chicago. Exhibited in 1933 at Chicago's Century-of-Progress International Exposition, it marked a radical departure from the heavy cast-iron models of earlier years with their crowded Victorian-era furnishings. The art moderne design featured streamlined windows tha: wrapped around the oval form with built-in window shades replacing the stuffy velvet curtains of the past. Neoclassical details such as the Greek key motif edging the ceiling and the carpeting and upholstery fabric adorned with wreathes, stars, and rosettes finished the interior. RIGHT A view of the Travel and Transportation Building, where the Pullman car was exhibited at the 1933 Century-of-Progress fair with its reflecting pool.

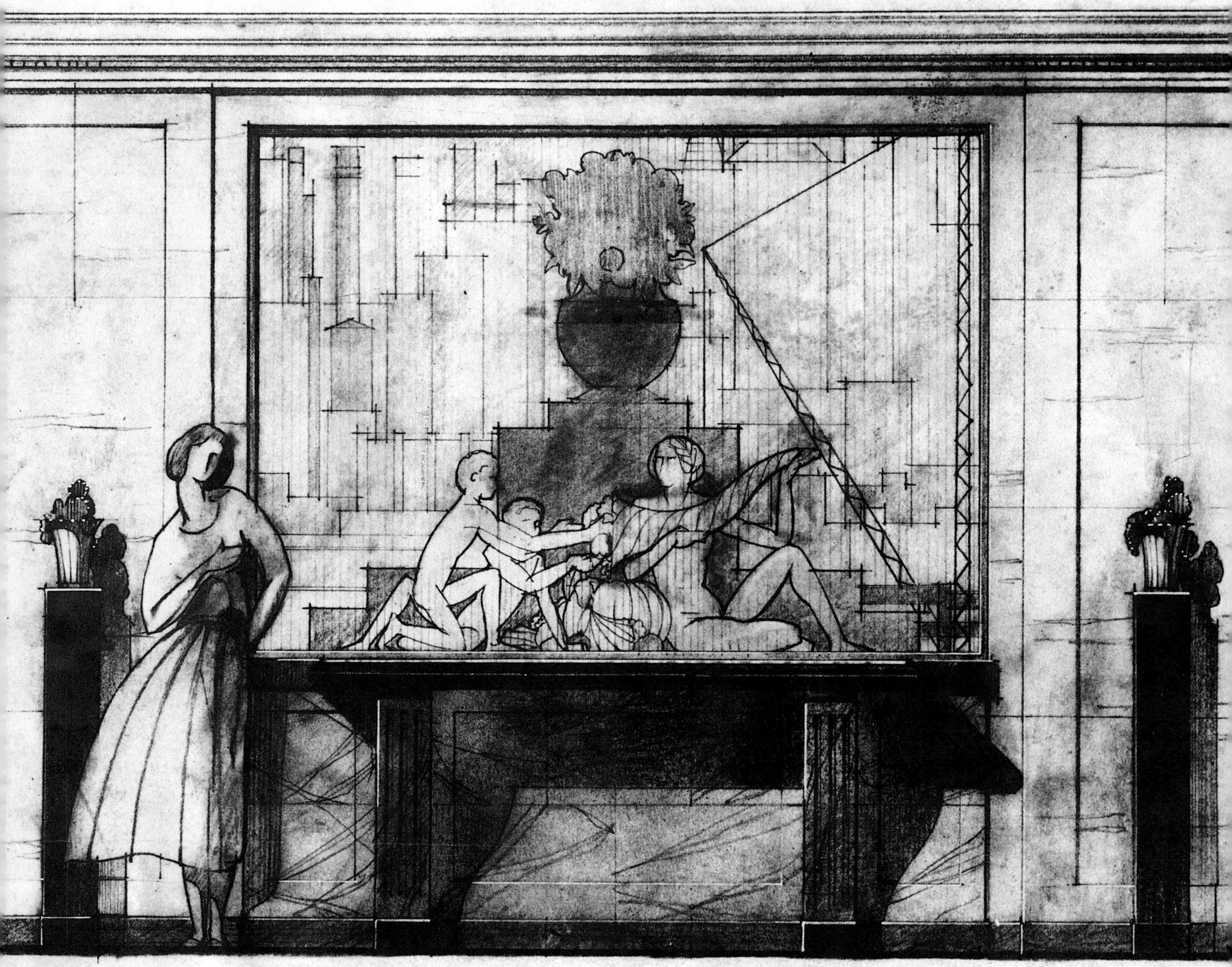

· SOVTH · WALL · OF · GROVND · FLOOR · LO

THESE PAGES In 1927, Marx designed the LaSalle Street offices in Chicago for A. G. Becker, an investment bank. The following year, the French artist Bernard Boutet de Monvel was commissioned to paint the mural, *Abundance Nourishing the Children of America*, for the art deco–style lobby, above. Boutet de Monvel, one of the many leading artists to exhibit at the Arts Club of Chicago, had a one-man show there in 1927. An original cartoon of the mural, opposite, illustrates how the proposed work would look in situ.

THESE PAGES As an associate architect for the Baxter Laboratories in Morton Grove, Illinois, Marx designed the reception lobby in 1949 with signature touches such as fossil stone walls, black terrazzo floors, and luxuriously modern custom-made furniture.

COMPLETE
SERVICE
DEPARTMEN
JACK'S
DEPT STORE

ABOVE AND RIGHT In 1952, Marx designed the site of the Alexander Hamilton Memorial in Chicago's Lincoln Park. A seventy-two-foot pylon of black granite rose above the elevated limestone plaza with a sculpture of Hamilton raised on a square plinth. In spite of a campaign by a small group of supporters to save it, the austere yet powerful structure was dismantled in 1993.

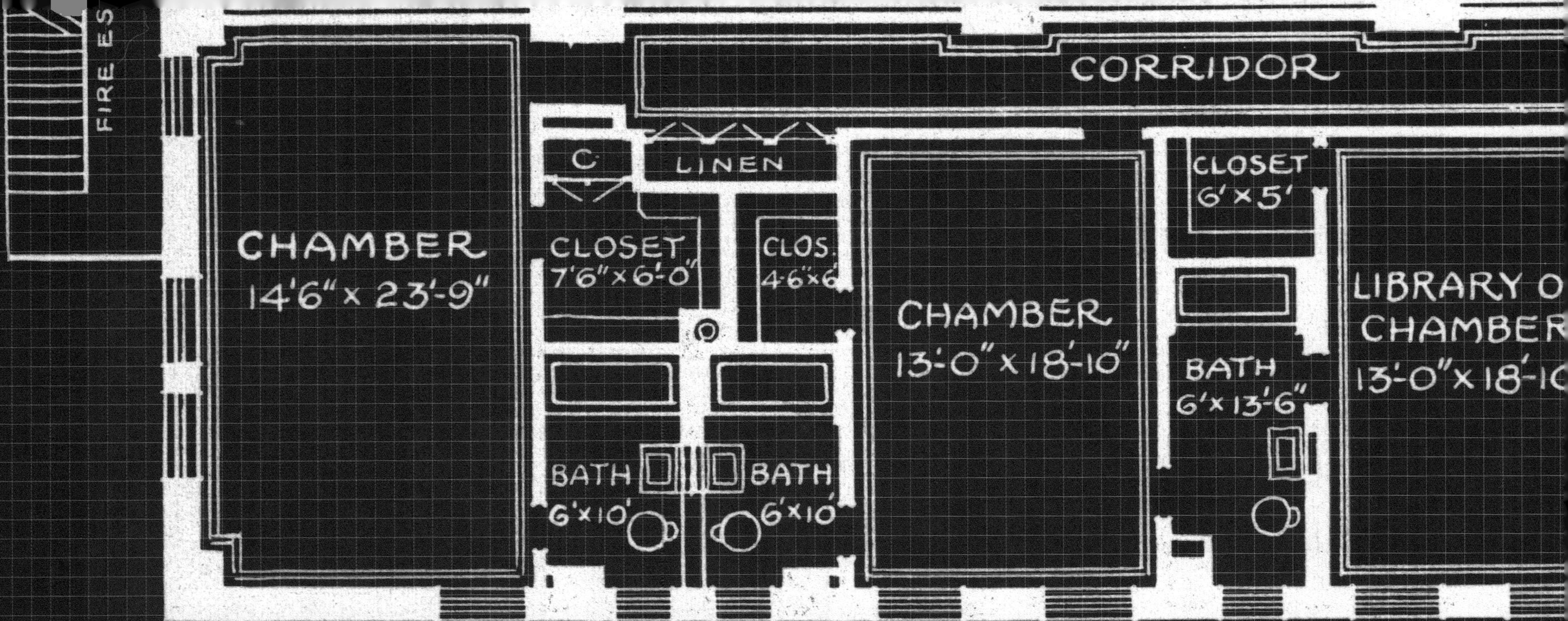

In the 1920s and 1930s Marx took on a number of residential projects wide-ranging in scope and decorative style. Most of these commissions were in Chicago or the North Shore suburbs where Marx and many of his clients had country homes. Having already designed several large houses for prominent residents such as advertising pioneer Albert D. Lasker and Julius Rosenwald, the head of the giant mail-order company Sears and Roebuck, the architect was hired to produce an impressive estate for Max Epstein. Its regal presence still graces its lakeside site in Winnetka, Illinois. Marx's versatility is evident in rooms outfitted with wood paneling, neoclassical details, and decorative Chinese wallpaper. His interest in the streamlined forms and industrial materials of modern design begins to emerge in his use of machine-age light fixtures, art deco–style fireplace surrounds, and subtly luxurious furniture of his own design.

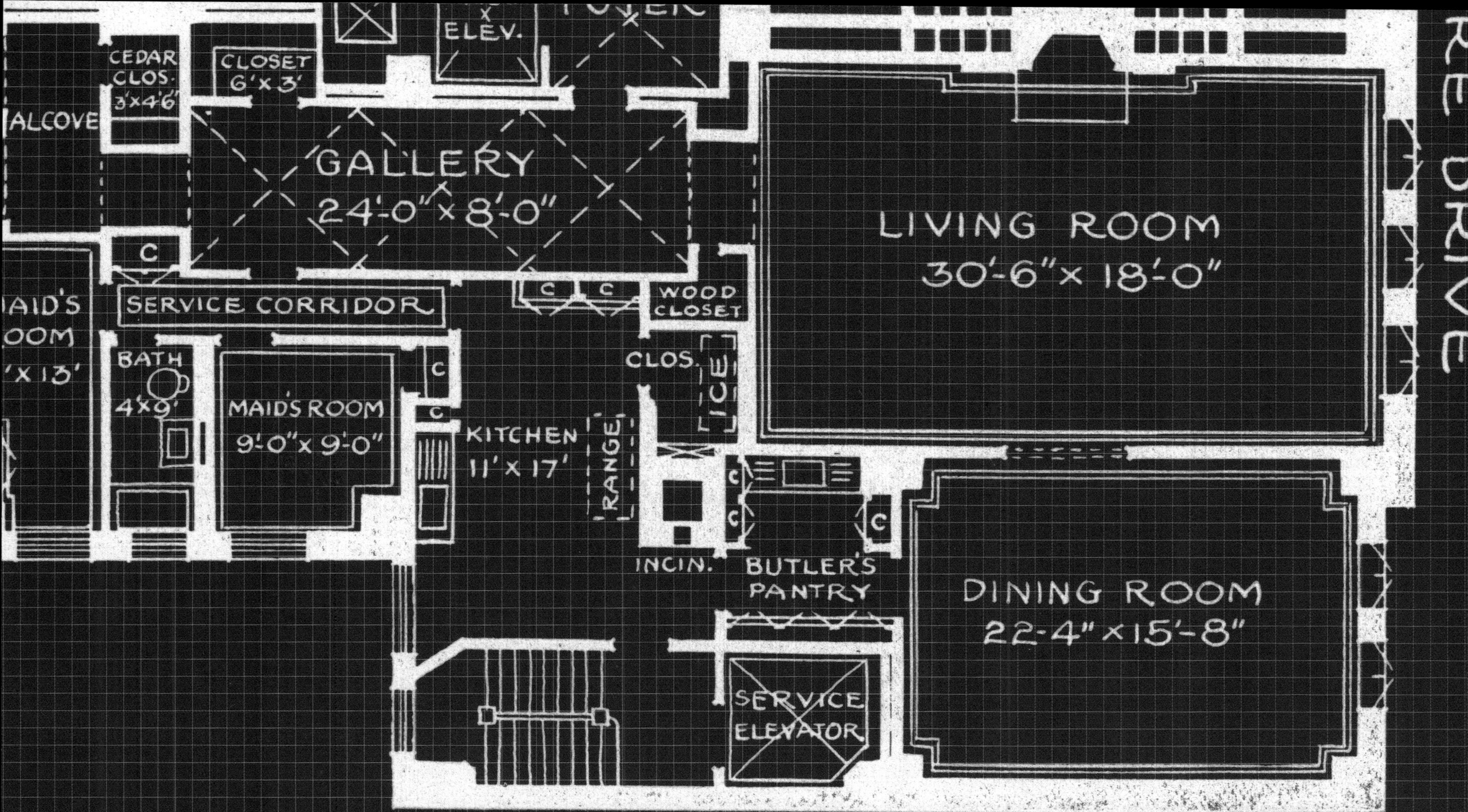

CHAPTER ONE

SETTLING IN

PROJECT

Floor plan of an apartment at 1540 North Lake Shore Drive, Chicago.
Building design by architects Huszagh and Hill, 1925.

SAMUEL A. MARX

ARCHITECT

333 N. MICHIGAN AVE. • CHICAGO, ILLINOIS

DATE	REVISED	JOB	DRAWING
1937		Mortimer B. Harris	

Marx's connection to Arthur Lehman, a member of New York's distinguished banking family, may well have been through the architect's first wife, Margaret Schaffner. In addition to running Hart, Schaffner and Marx, the men's clothier, the Schaffner family held a key interest in A.G. Becker, the Chicago investment firm whose offices Marx designed in the 1920s. Sears and Roebuck and the May Company department stores, two companies Marx had ties to, were among several large retail concerns financed by Lehman Brothers early in the twentieth century. Marx designed the interiors of the Lehman residence on East 70th Street in Manhattan that had been built in 1928 by prominent New York architect Aymar Embury II. The Lehmans, patrons of the Metropolitan Museum of Art and the newly formed Museum of the City of New York, had built an important collection of fifteenth- and sixteenth-century paintings and tapestries, many of which are now at the Metropolitan Museum of Art and the Fogg Museum of Art in Cambridge, Massachusetts. Marx, having demonstrated his ability to work with museum collections early in his career at the Isaac Delgado Museum of Art in New Orleans, proved adept at integrating the Lehmans' extraordinary art works into a well-appointed domestic setting. Marx went on to make this skill one of the hallmarks of his career. Cosmetics tycoon Estée Lauder bought the house in 1965 and lived there until her death in 2004. The family still owns the property.

LEFT As seen in turn-of-the-century interiors of Stanford White and others, the rooms in the four-story townhouse referenced a variety of period styles, a practice still in use in the 1920s. Ionic pilasters, carved plaster moldings, and a pedimented doorframe adorned the neoclassical limestone entry hall.

OPPOSITE One of the jewels of the collection, the fifteenth-century millefleurs tapestry, was hung in a large room with a Renaissance coffered ceiling. *Madonna and Child with Saint John the Baptist and an Angel*, an important tempera panel, is now in the collection of the Metropolitan Museum of Art in New York. Marx installed the Lehmans' Renaissance furniture in a fashion typical of leading art patrons at the time, such as Samuel H. Kress, whose Fifth Avenue residence featured many similar elements that had been removed from Venetian palazzi and shipped to the United States.

ABOVE Comfortable modern seating and a handsome collection of leather-bound books produced a relaxed, masculine air in the Lehmans' knotted pine–paneled library. Dentil moldings and a Greek key motif around the window frames supplied restrained decorative detail. A painting by Pierre-Auguste Renoir hung over the delicately carved fireplace.

ABOVE Marx produced a lighter, more feminine ambience in Adele Lewisohn Lehman's upstairs sitting room with its uncluttered furniture arrangement, light color palette, and rock crystal wall sconces by Baguès, a Paris firm that also had shops in New York.

LEFT Two zebra skin rugs add a fashionable touch to the entry hall, a small area leading to an enfilade of three large, high-ceilinged rooms: the library, the living room, and the dining room. Small pictures in tortoiseshell frames were above the staircase with its delicate faux-bamboo balustrade and carved glass newel post. A reeded circular column displayed a modern bust of a woman done in the classical style.

In 1934, Marx was commissioned to remodel the house belonging to Henry R. Levy overlooking Lake Michigan on Glade Road in Glencoe, Illinois. The house was originally designed around 1915 by the gifted architect Howard Van Doren Shaw for Moses Born, a wealthy Chicago businessman who served as the first president of Lake Shore Country Club. It was part of a cluster of four houses Shaw built for Born and each of his three children. Entered through twin gatehouses, the wooded enclave of the Born family compound, know locally as Bornly, epitomized country life in the lakeside community. Shaw, who, like Marx, had trained as an architect at the Massachusetts Institute of Technology, furnished stately homes for a distinguished North Shore clientele that included Edward Ryerson and the Donnelley family. His residential work, drawn largely on English and Italianate styles, and rendered in brick, fieldstone, and stucco, did much to set the foundation for the look and tone of these growing suburban communities. Marx, who was sixteen years Shaw's junior, took on a number of jobs to remodel Shaw houses in the 1930s.

ABOVE The library was paneled in pine flexwood with a limed finish. Two carved wall sconces with rock-crystal drops and a mirror hung over the simple slate fireplace surround. The parchment-clad demilune cabinets with Greek key decorations and low side tables by Marx were executed by the firm of William J. Quigley, Inc., the Chicago cabinetmaker. A pair of sculpted andirons, also by Marx, recalled the work of Alberto Giacometti for Jean-Michel Frank.

The house that belonged to Moses Born's daughter Florence and her husband, Harold E. Foreman, was built by Shaw in 1916 on the lakeside property of Bornly. Noted architect David Adler remodeled the house in 1920 after a fire nearly destroyed it. Marx was hired in the 1930s to update the design which was then featured in *Interior Design and Decoration* in April of 1941. In an article titled "A New Impetus to Modern Design," Marx's timeless appeal was described as having "the direct, straightforward spirit of today's design which will years from now still be attractive and in good taste."

ABOVE A Renoir was placed like a jewel on the deep violet walls of the living room. The baroque design of the fireplace surround, set squarely in a space devoid of architectural detailing such as molding or paneling, was inspired by the Parisian taste of the period seen in the work of designers like Serge Roche and Emilio Terry. Marx achieved a sense of balance in this sensual setting by countering the hard surface of the Victoria Blue marble of the fireplace with plush carpeting and oyster-white velvet upholstery. Marx combined his own furniture designs, such as the parchment coffee table, with antique pieces he had selected to complement the scheme.

OPPOSITE A pair of silver-leafed doors opened from the dining room onto the entryway. The floor, of ivory and dark brown travertine, was set off by bright white walls. The wood handrail of the staircase was lacquered in a faux-malachite finish; the newels were finished in chrome. A brown clipped-fur runner on the staircase hinted at the unexpectedly sumptuous interiors of the urbane summer residence.

LEFT The enclosed porch made the most of the house's superb lakeside site. Large floor-to-ceiling double-hung windows let in abundant daylight and gave views of the grounds and Lake Michigan. The open-air ambience was accentuated by the use of bamboo shades and a floor of blue-gray ceramic tiles inlaid with silver. A pair of French doors flanked the pale-yellow porcelain stove. Formal openwork transoms above the louvered wood doors related to the curvilinear features of the adjoining living room.

OPPOSITE A Georgian-style oval mirror floated in front of a curtained window in the powder room. Painted silver paper, a mirrored vanity, and a mosaic-tiled floor contributed to the opulent atmosphere of the house.

RIGHT Marx lined the walls of the dining room in kappa shells, a material he used frequently for their soft ivory-colored luster. A crystal chandelier and silver leaf torchières placed in the corners enhanced the candlelit mood. The modern Aubusson carpet in shades of cream and café au lait offset the iridescent sheen of the walls.

Around 1920, Marx built an unassuming Colonial-style house for himself at 1140 Sheridan Road in Glencoe, near the Lake Shore Country Club, the social hub of the well-to-do German-Jewish community that had established summer residences in the still-rustic North Shore area. Although the house was large, its discreet character hardly rivaled the grand properties of Marx's titan-of-industry clients, many of whom also had homes nearby. Every August, Marx hosted a birthday party for himself that was attended by family, friends, and fellow architects, including John Holabird and Mies van der Rohe. Marx kept the house, spending summers and weekends there, until 1962 when he and his wife, Florene, moved to New York City.

RIGHT The six-bedroom wood-shingled house with its twin bay windows, plantation shutters, and cedar shake roof stood on a lot just under an acre in size. With three maids' rooms and an intercom system, Marx lived a lifestyle lavish by standards of the day yet very much in keeping with his social set. The naturalistic grounds of the Marx house contrasted with the extensive formal gardens of his neighbors, particularly the Stonehill and Bensinger estates across the road. In later years, Marx placed a Marino Marini bronze sculpture of a man on horseback, now in the collection of the Art Institute of Chicago, in the back garden amid parterres, vineyards, and a small pond.

OPPOSITE The living room, with its plastered walls and crown molding, was furnished with traditional period furniture. The bookcases, the étagère stacked with bound volumes, the leather wing chair, and the floor lamp call to mind Marx's love of reading. A classical bronze bust stood in the foreground.

RIGHT The symmetrical treatment of the living room was centered on a simple black fireplace surround with a neoclassical pediment adorned with palmettes. An architect's drafting table sat in the middle of the room, which was arranged to provide comfortable areas for reading and drawing, recalling Thomas Jefferson's cabinet at Monticello with its reading chair, rotating book table, and standing desk.

BELOW RIGHT A neoclassical vitrine in black lacquer mirrored the fireplace on the facing wall in the doublewide living room typical of the Greek Revival houses Marx knew from his childhood in Natchez, Mississippi. The architect, a talented draftsman and amateur artist, painted the two watercolors flanking the cabinet.

RIGHT The neoclassical theme continued in the dining room, where Federal-era details such as the fan motif on the fireplace and the stars edging the ceiling were successfully worked into a twentieth-century setting. The striped window shades, used throughout the house, added a tailored sense of consistency to the interiors. The white walls and geometric pattern of the curtains gave the room a modern air and hinted at the future direction of Marx's work.

EDGECLIFF

Marx designed Edgecliff, a stately residence on a high bluff in Winnetka, Illinois, overlooking Lake Michigan, in 1930 for Max Epstein, the founder of Chicago's General American Tank Car Corporation. The exterior of the mansion, modeled on an eighteenth-century French chateau, with its perfect symmetry and orderly fenestration, recalls Mill Road Farm, the house David Adler built for Albert D. Lasker in Lake Forest, Illinois, five years earlier. The two architects were influenced by their Beaux-Arts training and the great houses of France they, like others of their generation, would have seen while touring the continent. Rather than drawing a direct quotation from European precedent, Marx produced a modern take on an historical model, grafting design elements from various sources and paring down forms to create a contemporary effect. The estate was later owned by another Chicago businessman, Nathan Cummings, who made it a showplace for his collection of Impressionist and Postimpressionist paintings.

PREVIOUS PAGES The approach to Edgecliff, with its twin gatehouses and allée of elm trees, made for a grand entrance. The main house, of whitewashed brick with black shutters and hip roof, was joined by two perfectly symmetrical single-story wings.

OPPOSITE Regency style outbuildings, like the small folly-like cabana with its pagoda roof and oculus windows, dotted the nine-acre site. Closely-mown grass framed the swimming pool in the formal grounds by landscape designer Mrs. Walter Brewster, which included clipped hedges and garden statuary.

RIGHT The grandly proportioned library, perfectly circular in plan, with a silver leaf coved ceiling, drew on French directoire and Federal era details. Attenuated columns topped with acanthus leaves, gilded rosettes, and a crystal-beaded chandelier provided an elegant backdrop for comfortable leather- and velvet-covered seating. A round Aubusson carpet completed the scene of a room whose formal gravity made a princely impression.

OPPOSITE The well-ordered plan of the entry hall was nicely balanced by the graceful sweep of the staircase. A series of arched doorways led to the elegant rooms on the ground floor.

RIGHT Epstein was a renowned collector of old-master paintings and a long-standing trustee of the Art Institute of Chicago. Works by Titian, Rubens, Van Dyck, Velasquez, and El Greco were expertly incorporated into the interiors of this formal residence. Integrating museum-quality masterpieces into a domestic setting was a strength of Marx's, whose skills as an architect were enhanced by his superb eye for art. The paneled walls of the living room provided a dignified backdrop for such works as Botticelli's *Virgin and Child with Angel,* which was over the fireplace.

BELOW RIGHT The Dutch portrait of a man hung in the light formal dining room. A crystal beaded chandelier added charm to the neo-classical setting detailed with fluted Corinthian pilasters and dentil moldings. A pair of wing chairs and a pedestal table were placed in the demilune bay of double-hung windows oriented toward the lake.

OPPOSITE The Chinese painted paper in the powder room reflects the 1930s taste for chinoiserie. Fashionable interiors by designers such as Elsie de Wolfe, Syrie Maugham, and Frances Elkins made use of these decorative papers in some of the most memorable rooms of the period. The revival of interest in this kind of wallpaper may well have been due, in part, to the widely publicized opening in 1924 of the American Wing at the Metropolitan Museum of Art in New York. The Early American period rooms in the new wing, particularly the Philadelphia Room and the Alexandria Alcove, featured Chinese wallpaper and demonstrated for the twentieth-century viewer a timeless chic and suitability. The New York firm of Charles R. Gracie and Sons was a popular source for such papers and a favorite supplier of Marx's, who continued to use these treatments throughout his career.

ABOVE The upstairs bath had silvered walls trimmed in steel and glass and was outfitted with modern fixtures. The Moroccan rug added texture and an unexpected counterpoint to these sleek surfaces.

In the 1930s, Marx designed three apartments at 1540 North Lake Shore Drive for Mr. and Mrs. Frank Mayer, Mr. and Mrs. P. D. Block, Jr., and Mr. and Mrs. Mortimer B. Harris, all of whom were social acquaintances of Marx from summering in the North Shore suburbs. Built by Huszagh and Hill in 1925, the seventeen-story stone and red-brick structure towered over its neighboring townhouses on this northern stretch of the drive and was widely noted for its most famous resident, P. K. Wrigley, who occupied the triplex penthouse. The building had roughly thirty twelve-room apartments, two per floor, each with two or more maids' rooms large kitchens, and stunning views of the lake. As he would do with other city apartments, Marx left these well-functioning floor plans largely unchanged and furnished the interiors with wood-paneled libraries, stylish fireplace surrounds, and an intriguing mix of period pieces and modern furniture of his own design.

ABOVE AND OPPOSITE The unusual Chinese painted paper in the living room set the sophisticated tone of the apartment. The Chippendale-style mirror continued the chinoiserie theme of the living room and balanced out the ornate carving of the facing fireplace surround.

LEFT Deep coral provided the background for a classic oriental scene rendered in black and white, or *en grisaille*. This type of Chinese paper was normally painted in a bright, multicolored palette. Marx's uncommon choice revealed his erudition and restraint and imbued the room with an air of refined distinction. Chinese ceramic figures were placed on the carved-wood mantle. Scenes of flowering trees, peonies, cranes, and poppy flowers bring a gracious sense of movement and fantasy to the large room which is still intact today.

OPPOSITE TOP AND BOTTOM The waterfall-style coffee table in the living room was executed by Quigley in parchment with a lacquered Coromandel panel set into the top.

OPPOSITE The highly unusual design of the carved marble fireplace surround is the focus of the subdued treatment of the dining room.

ABOVE The carved openwork mirror frame serves as overmantle and faces the view of the lake from the dining room, as it did decades ago.

ABOVE The original Chippendale-style dining table and chairs may well have been made by Quigley, whose workrooms produced many quality reproductions of period furniture for designers like Marx, David Adler, and Ernest A. Grunsfeld, Jr. The glass ceiling fixture is American, furnished by M. A. Van Esso, who had a shop in Chicago.

ABOVE The limed wood paneling of the library was edged in a simple molding carved with a stylized key motif. A pair of arched concave niches displayed a collection of majolica.

OPPOSITE The current residents have kept the spirit of the room intact, filling the niches with their collection of blue and white Chinese ceramics pottery and introducing a secretary similar to the one that was there originally.

Designed by Shaw in 1909 for Benjamin Bensinger, the head of the Brunswick Bowling and Billiards company, the Italianate house on Lake Michigan was remodeled by Marx in 1936 when Bensinger's son, Robert, and his family took residence there. Marx left the original floor plan untouched and updated the existing spaces with fresh and imaginative decorative details. The red-oak floors were replaced with black and brown terrazzo, and the heavy oak paneling was limed throughout to lighten the rooms.

ABOVE The walls of the entry hall were smoothed with crisp, white plaster. The gentle S-curves of the sculpted wall sconces contrast nicely with a pair of Regency armchairs.

OPPOSITE While the house is now occupied by its third owner, many of the decorative details, such as the sconces, remain intact.

ABOVE Marx transformed the room that was originally designed for the game of billiards into a cozy library. The architect replaced the brick-faced fireplace surround with a neoclassical design in black-and-white marble. The hand-painted Chinese wallpaper depicted famous American landmarks such as the Capitol Building in Washington, D.C., Niagara Falls, and Columbus Circle in New York City, in an oriental landscape. The effect of these naïve and unexpected juxtapositions is both surrealistic and delightful.

OPPOSITE AND OVERLEAF Still in place today, the wallpaper is as unusual and vibrant as it was over seventy years ago.

A HISTORY OF THE MODERN WORLD

RIGHT The downstairs bar, with its avant-garde ceiling fixture and zebra skin rugs, was a playful take on the art moderne–style of the day. Tubular aluminum barstools and other pieces by Warren McArthur were placed in a graphic setting of black, white, and red. Edgar Miller, a Chicago artist who collaborated with Marx on numerous commissions, executed a mural of humorous hunting scenes for the curvilinear walls. The reverse-painted images on the mirrors behind the bar depicted scenes of billiards and bowling that made reference to the family's business.

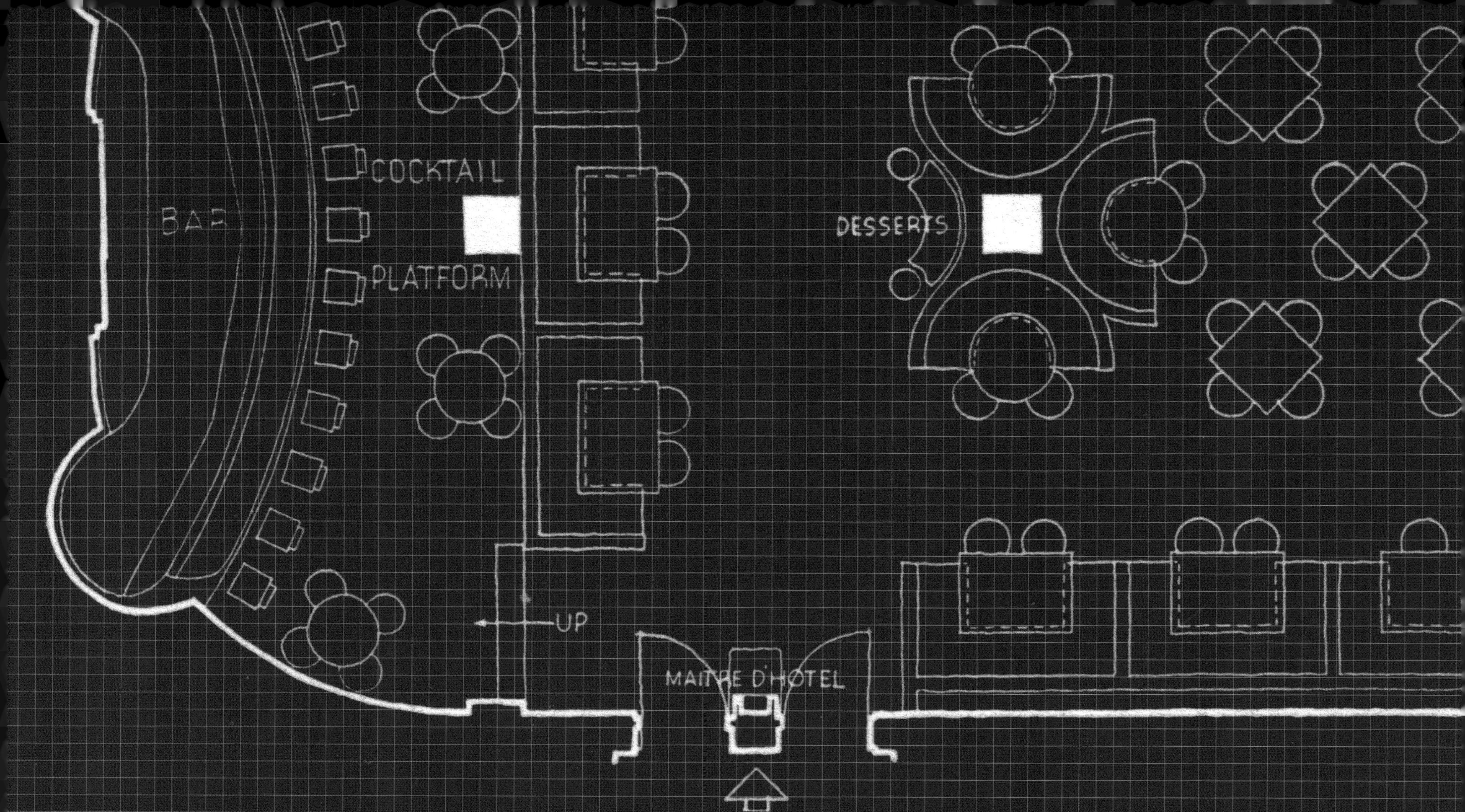

Marx's first known essay into the design of hotel restaurants was the Pump Room in the Ambassador East Hotel in Chicago, still remembered as the epitome of glamorous, see-and-be-seen dining rooms in the days of Café Society. Its tremendous success launched the architect's career as a much-sought-after creator of distinctive public spaces whose Midas touch ensured favorable press and in-the-black ledger books. Socially active and well liked for his quick wit, Marx belonged to many private clubs and was called on to design lounges and dining rooms for the Tavern Club, where he had been a charter member, and the Arts Club of Chicago. Marx brought the same allure of his clubrooms to a wider audience through his designs for movie houses and the Fred Harvey restaurants in Chicago train stations. Over twenty years, J. Paul Getty hired Marx to design several public rooms at the Hotel Pierre in New York. In 1957, Getty, a dream client for the imaginative architect, tapped him to design the Pierre Marques Hotel, an upscale resort on Getty's secluded property in Acapulco, Mexico.

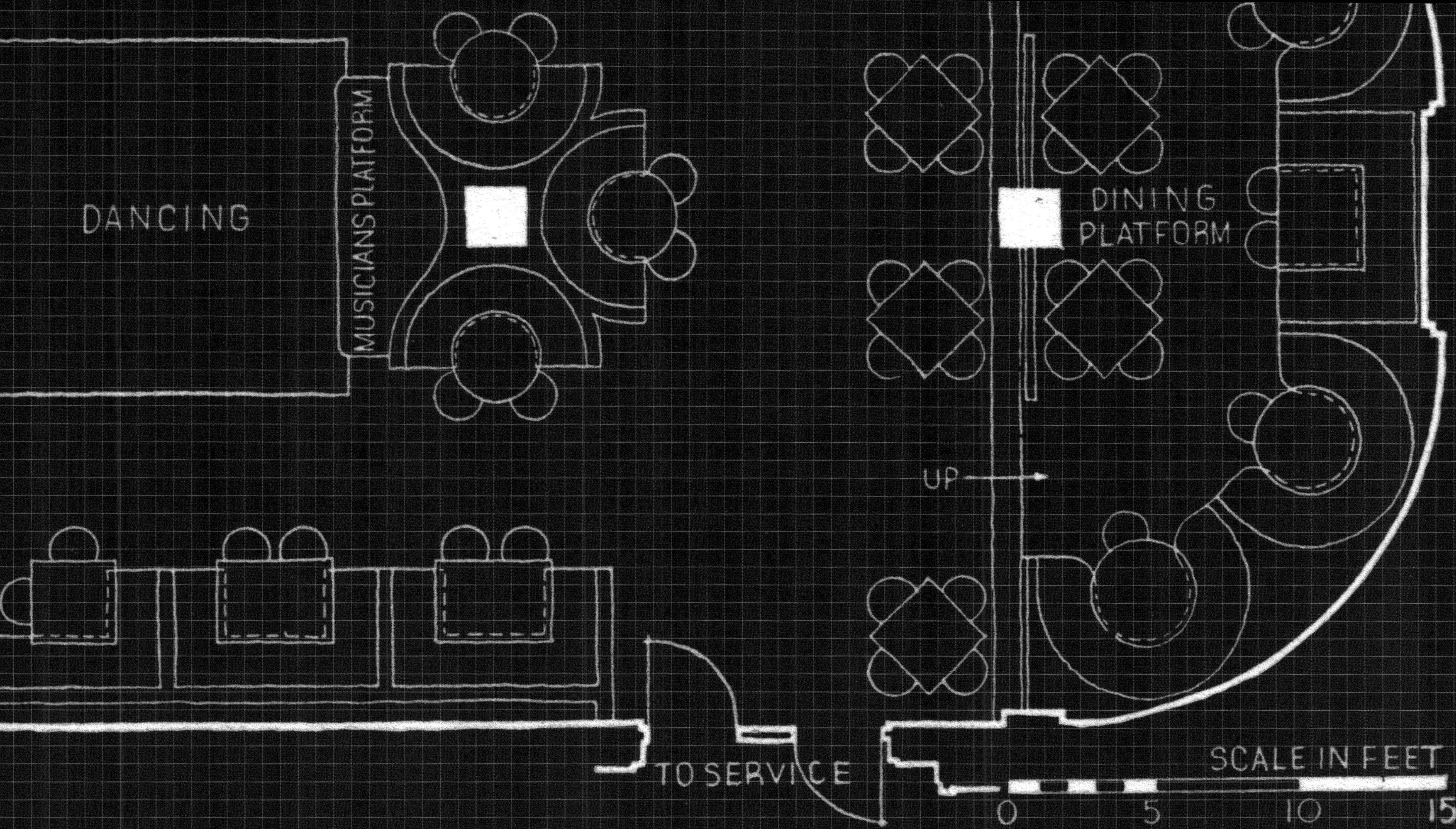

CHAPTER TWO

CAFE SOCIETY

PROJECT

Floor plan for the Pump Room at the Ambassador East Hotel, Chicago.

SAMUEL A. MARX • NOEL L. FLINT • CHARLES W. SCHONNE
ARCHITECTS
333 NORTH MICHIGAN AVENUE • CHICAGO, ILLINOIS

DATE	REVISED	JOB	DRAWING
1938		Ernest Byfield	

When the Pump Room opened in the fall of 1938, it caused an instant sensation. Located in the luxurious Ambassador East Hotel in the center of Chicago's Gold Coast, it set a new standard for fashionable supper clubs and brought Marx widespread acclaim. Many other hotel owners, eager to duplicate the commercial success of the Pump Room, sought him out to produce similarly seductive environments in such places as the Hotel Pierre in New York. Much of the Pump Room's cachet came from its glamorous movie-star clientele.

Named for its eighteenth-century predecessor in Bath, England, where British aristocracy mingled with stage actors, the Pump Room was the favorite stopping-off point for Hollywood personalities traveling from New York to California by train in the days before air travel. Passengers boarded the storied Twentieth Century Limited at Grand Central Station in the evening and arrived on the luxury express the following morning at LaSalle Street Station. Travelers spent the day in Chicago shopping at Marshall Field's and lunching at the Pump Room before leaving for the West Coast in the evening.

The impeccable setting of the Pump Room, with its back-lit banquettes and dramatically garbed wait staff, provided the dream photo opportunity for film studios seeking publicity for their stars. Photographers were on staff to document the appearances of such celebrities as Elizabeth Taylor, Natalie Wood and Robert Wagner, and Frank Sinatra. Portable white telephones were shuttled to tables and guests advised the maitre d' if they were expecting calls or a telegram.

LEFT The plumed headdress and satin coat of the doorman were emblems of the famed supper club, known for its unique panache.

OPPOSITE Tableside service, conducted with theatrical flair, added to the Pump Room's renown. Ernest Byfield, owner of the Ambassador Hotels, was a showman of the first order who believed in dazzling guests with a memorable dining experience.

OVERLEAF Deep cobalt-blue walls, white leather banquettes, and delicate crystal light fixtures produced an unforgettable effect. Low lamps at each table and custom table settings further added to the seductive atmosphere.

Founded in 1927, seven years into Prohibition, the Tavern, as it was originally known, stated as its purpose "to encourage the arts, intellectual recreation, and good-humored interest in life." With prominent Chicago cultural figures such as Carl Sandburg and Frank Lloyd Wright, as well as Marx, among its members, the club embodied the blithe attitude taken toward the Volstead Act in major American cities. Perched on the twenty-fifth and twenty-sixth floors of the newly erected Holabird & Root skyscraper at 333 North Michigan Avenue, the club enjoyed dramatic city views and outdoor terraces. Notable Chicago architectural firms, including Samuel A. Marx and Holabird & Root, established their offices at this prestigious address. The interiors of the Tavern Club celebrated the city's artistic flair by showcasing murals by John W. Norton and Edgar Miller, some of which are still intact. The dining room and lounge area, originally designed by WPA artist Winold Reis, were updated by Marx in the 1930s.

LEFT The north dining room, where members met for lunch, had a low-key, masculine air. The side chairs, with their square cutout backs and metal handles, are a Marx trademark. The serving tables are faced in malachite-colored Di Noc, an early experimental laminate developed by the 3M company.

LEFT The gently curved back wall, glazed emerald green, is set off by dove-gray leatherette banquettes and a plaster ceiling.

OPPOSITE Desert scenes of sculpted cacti rendered in plaster could have been a wry commentary on the Tavern Club's origins during drier days.

RIGHT Flexwood, a product developed by the U.S. Plywood Corporation as an alternative to old-fashioned wood paneling, covered the walls in the lounge, where recessed circular ceiling fixtures and table lamps provided ambient light. Marx used the material, which came in easily installed sheets, extensively in both residential and commercial projects. Comfortable seating areas were furnished with leather sofas and glass-topped tables designed by Marx.

RECORD
TOWN & COUNTRY

The Arts Club of Chicago has played a vital role in the city's cultural scene since it was founded in 1916, just three years after the Art Institute of Chicago's historic Armory Show. Its purpose of bringing contemporary works of art to Chicago was carried out with impressive rigor, prescience, and style. From its inception, the Arts Club exhibited works by Paul Cézanne, André Derain, Henri Matisse, Marcel Duchamp, and many other pioneering European and American artists. Concerts and lectures were given by Igor Stravinsky, Gertrude Stein, and Bertrand Russell.

This access to the best of the new and the avant-garde had a profound influence on the tastes and collecting habits of Chicago's art-minded elite, and was, no doubt, of great interest to Marx, a longtime member. In 1935, the Arts Club moved to spacious new quarters in the South Tower of the Wrigley Building on Michigan Avenue. Arthur Heun, who had been the architect for the club's two previous spaces, designed the plan for the new two-story location. Marx, who served on the club's board of directors at the time, designed the second-floor dining room.

ABOVE AND OPPOSITE The Arts Club dining room, which opened in 1937, was defined by a large oval cove recessed in the ceiling and extensive sculpted plasterwork. The highly imaginative treatment of the fireplace surround and the fringed, swag-form window treatments reflected the preference for fantasy and the baroque at the time. The playful yet graceful wall sconces recall similar models used by Marx at the Bensinger house just one year earlier. The seminal show, Fantastic Art, Dada and Surrealism, which opened the previous year at the Museum of Modern Art in New York and traveled to several American cities, popularized the application of these animated forms in fashion and interior design.

ABOVE Many of the baroque flourishes Marx had used in the soigné dining rooms of the Pump Room and the Arts Club lent themselves nicely to the Hollywood-style glamour Marx brought to his designs for the Lamar Theater in Oak Park, Illinois.

RIGHT The lobby, with its marbleized walls, tufted white leather benches, and plaster wall sconces whose feather-like leaf forms extended to the ceiling, made the fantasy of a 1930s movie set accessible to the general public.

Beginning in the late nineteenth century, and working in partnership with the Santa Fe Railway line, Fred Harvey, and later his two sons, established a group of hotels and restaurants along the southwestern route to service the growing number of tourists traveling by train to the West Coast. By the mid 1930s, with dozens of locations and slogans boasting "3,000 Miles of Hospitality" and "Fred Harvey All the Way!" the company had effectively fashioned itself into an early precursor to the chain restaurants prevalent in American life today. In 1939, following the success of the Pump Room, Marx was hired to design a new restaurant for Fred Harvey in Chicago's Dearborn Station to accommodate travelers and local businesses in the Loop. Marx replaced the small existing lunchroom with a complex of four luxuriously modern rooms that brought the sophisticated atmosphere of the architect's private clubs to a broader audience.

ABOVE Marx set the mood for the journey west with earthy tones of red and terracotta accented by touches of gleaming chrome and glass. Custom-designed barstools in steel, sanded oak, and leather lined the serpentine bar of the cocktail lounge.

ABOVE Machine-age light fixtures in circular coves cast an ambient light over the posh dining room. Marx repeated these forms in the round niches displaying cacti sculpted in plaster. Miller supplied the amusing mural depicting scenes of early Chicago settlers.

RIGHT Curvilinear shapes and indirect lighting from the ceiling cove and bar area gave the cocktail lounge an air of cool sophistication.

When billionaire industrialist J. Paul Getty purchased the Hotel Pierre in New York in 1938, he promptly turned to Marx to breathe new life into the faltering Fifth Avenue institution. Over the following twenty years, Marx designed several of the public spaces in the upscale hotel, turning it into one of Manhattan's most glamorous destinations.

LEFT AND OPPOSITE
The central rotunda of the Hotel Pierre, which, although much changed, still exists today, is an oval-shaped room with two sweeping staircases leading to the Grand Ballroom. The space featured bold architectural gestures often used by Marx in the late 1930s, such as the wide sculpted moldings of the doorways and the large circular ceiling cove. A multi-tiered plaster chandelier hung in the center of the room, adding a baroque flourish.

ABOVE AND OPPOSITE Curved, tufted settees and Regency side chairs encircled the delightful cocktail tables, which had legs shaped like seahorses. Decorative panels of painted paper wrapped the walls of the rotunda in scenes of Manhattan Island, with its waterways, bridges, parks, and city buildings as well as water towers and smoke stacks.

"Red, White and Baroque" trumpeted the pages of *Interiors* when the Hotel Pierre's Cotillion Room opened in 1941. Marx, re-creating the fashionable supper-club scene of the Pump Room, this time turned for inspiration to the romance of the bygone plantation days of his native South. The sculpted white balustrades and delicate crystal light fixtures contrasted with the deep vermillion walls of the high-ceilinged dining room.

RIGHT Large murals by Miller in cartouche-shaped frames made light of the decorous courtship rituals of the American South.

ABOVE With the success of the Cotillion Room firmly established, Marx was called back to the Hotel Pierre to design the Pierre Grill and lobby area. The ultramodern lobby featured curved walls sheathed in limed oak. Generously proportioned armchairs, side chairs, and stools, upholstered in a chenille and metallic yarn fabric by Dorothy Liebes, were juxtaposed with simple, cylinder-shaped cocktail tables. A long, horizontal gilt-wood and lacquered panel by Miller made a playful show of the history of the American table: scenes of Cortez and Montezuma, the first Thanksgiving, and George Washington's troops at Valley Forge were all rendered in the artist's signature tongue-in-cheek style.

OPPOSITE The Pierre Grill demonstrated Marx's supreme skill in designing public spaces. The bold geometric shapes, deliberate use of materials, and balance of form and surface decoration emerged as unmistakable elements of his work. The modern room, absent of architectural ornament, achieved a serene sense of balance through the repeating pattern of the fossil stone walls and the pinwheel-like arrangement of the banquettes as they circled the columns. Conceived as a more casual lunchtime alternative to the Cotillion Room, the Grill featured an open stainless-steel kitchen, visible from the dining room. The pared-down, classical columns are adorned with historical scenes executed by Miller in a *sgraffito*, or scratchwork, technique. The muralist also created the bas-relief panels depicting scenes from antiquity.

Marx's last public commission was the design of the Pierre Marques Hotel in Acapulco, Mexico. Built in 1957 on land owned by J. Paul Getty and adjacent to his own private retreat, the Pierre Marques signaled the emergence of Acapulco as the resort of choice for international socialites and Hollywood personalities. Marx, along with Wolfgang Schoenborn, the local project architect, built a series of large modern buildings joined by open-air passageways on the 480-acre oceanfront site. The German-born Schoenborn, a Mexican citizen, would marry Florene Marx after her husband's death in 1964, and the couple made Acapulco their home.

PREVIOUS PAGES A rendering of the Pierre Marques Hotel gives a bird's-eye view of the rectilinear arrangement of the connected buildings, which faced the beach and surrounded a kidney-shaped swimming pool.

LEFT Stone walls in shades of beige, rose, and gray defined the structures. Openwork grids of cast stone and the gently pitched terracotta roofs were natural adaptations of a modern architectural idiom to the tropical climate. Marx reduced the austerity of these forms through his expert use of color and his deft, organic application of materials.

LEFT Marx employed repetition, asymmetry, and strong horizontal lines to produce a harmonious result. The overhang of the roof and deep setbacks of the individual guest suites allowed for shade throughout the day.

OPPOSITE A large expanse of glass enclosed the dining room, which overlooked a rectangular water garden that also served as a reflecting pool.

ABOVE A vintage brochure promised that a visit to this "world-famous resort is like being an honored guest at a tropical estate." Landscaped grounds, lush gardens, swimming pools, and easy access to the beach made the Pierre Marques a luxurious vacation spot.

RIGHT A free-form canopy extended over the swimming pool that was nestled between the two interlocking wings of the building.

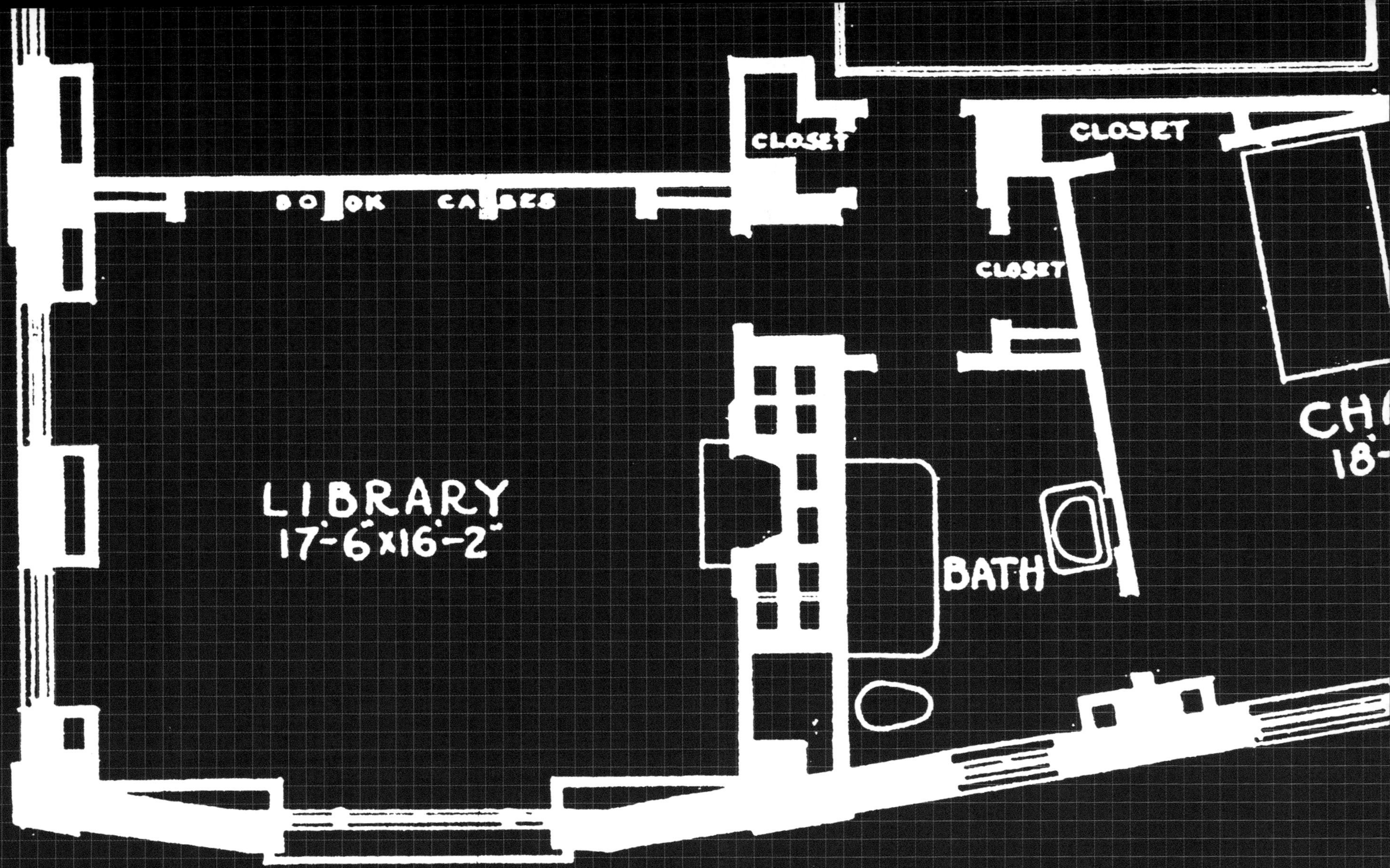

After Marx's marriage to Florene May Straus in 1937, the couple moved to 1325 North Astor Street, the premier 1928 apartment building by Rebori, Dewey and Wentworth in Chicago's Near North Side. Marx went straight to work designing the couple's floor-through residence in the direct, modern style that came to define his later work. As his own best client, he developed a model of high-end modern living that blended architecture, design, and fine art into a rich yet user-friendly environment. In 1939, the Marxes attended the Golden Gate Exposition in San Francisco and made several purchases from its Decorative Arts Division, which had been organized by textile designer Dorothy Liebes. Marx forged lasting working relationships with several designers exhibiting at the fair, including Liebes, William Haines, and Stanislav V'Soske.

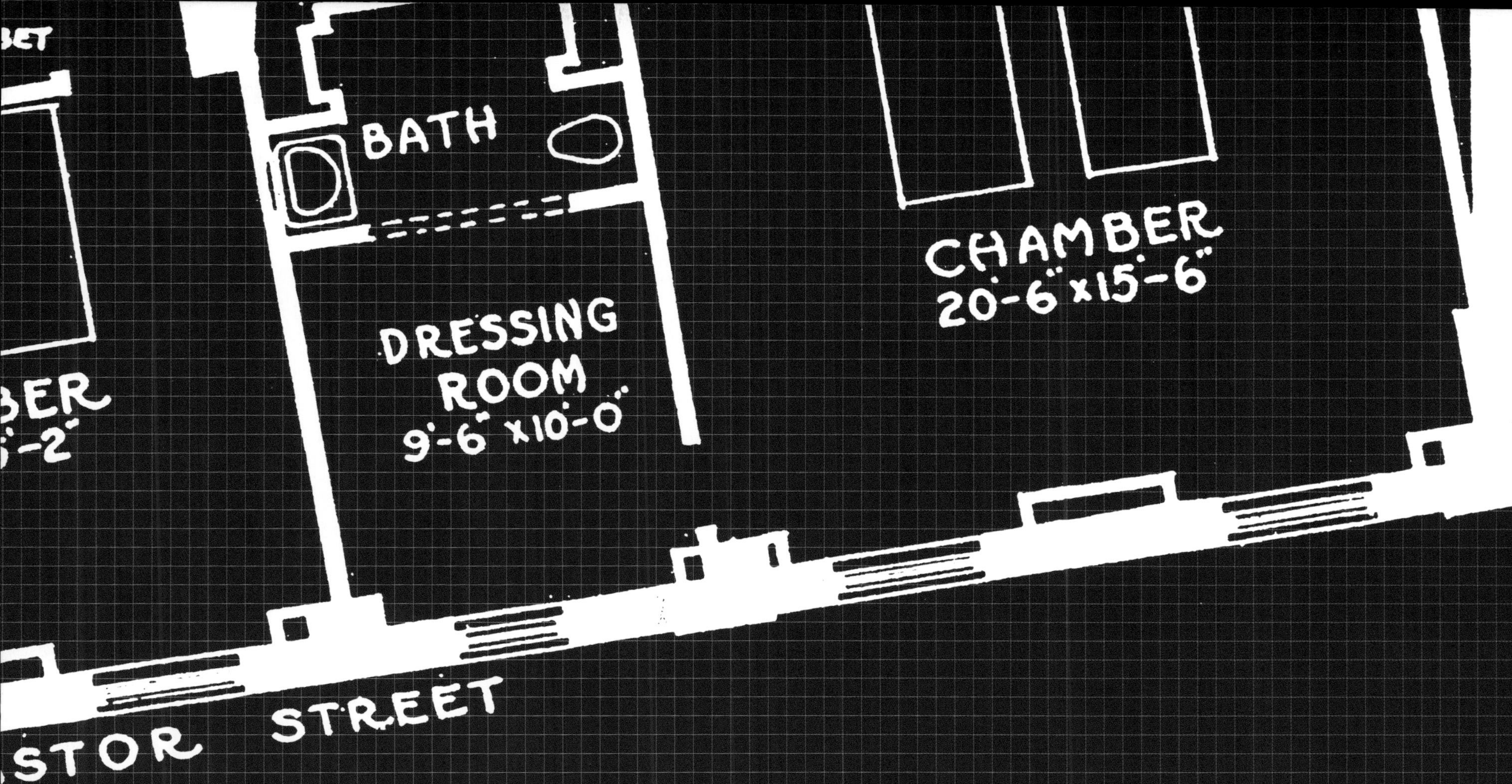

CHAPTER THREE

FLORENE AND SAM AT HOME

PROJECT

Floor plan of apartment at 1325 Astor Street, Chicago.

SAMUEL A. MARX • NOEL L. FLINT • CHARLES W. SCHONNE
ARCHITECTS
333 NORTH MICHIGAN • CHICAGO, ILLINOIS

DATE	REVISED	JOB	DRAWING
1939		Samuel A. Marx	

LEFT The entryway of the Marxes' unmistakably modern apartment was striking in its clarity and simplicity. Black terrazzo floors and white, minimally detailed walls produced a crisp, high-contrast background to the carefully chosen furnishings. Two black leather chairs, designed by Hollywood actor turned interior decorator William Haines and featured in his Desert Living Room at the 1939 Golden Gate Exposition in San Francisco, were by the front door. The area rug, produced by French textile expert Marie Cuttoli after a painting by Miró, also purchased at the fair, enlivened the space with biomorphic forms and vigorous shots of color.

ABOVE The console table, with its convex base and circular cutout, anchored the space with its simple geometric forms. Two cube-shaped wall sconces in painted metal, hung on either side of the Chinese stone rubbing, provided indirect light.

OPPOSITE Braque's 1936 *Woman Seated at an Easel*, with its central field of golden daylight and its richly layered composition, indicated the audacious direction the Marxes' collection took in the decade after the couple moved to North Astor Street. A large, semitransparent sculpture by Russian constructivist Naum Gabo occupied the semicircular niche.

In 1937, Marx married Florene May Straus, the daughter of David May, founder of the May Company department stores. Her previous marriage to Martin L. Straus II, with whom she had two children, had ended in divorce. The couple moved to 1325 North Astor Street, where the spare but luxuriously detailed interiors Marx created, with the help of some of the country's most innovative craftsmen, were no doubt an impressive calling card for future commissions. Not surprisingly, his design also turned out to be the ideal backdrop for the couple's daringly modern art works.

The Marxes did not originally set out to build an art collection, but in 1939, with their new apartment nearly completed, they attended the Golden Gate Exposition in San Francisco, where they fell in love with Georges Braque's 1935 *Yellow Tablecloth* and purchased it on the spot. Upon their return to Chicago, Marx plunged headlong into seeking out top-notch pieces by the artists of the School of Paris he admired, and quickly added several important works by Henri Matisse, Pablo Picasso, and Constantin Brancusi. Many of these purchases were made through Pierre Matisse, the artist's son and the New York art dealer whose legendary gallery represented artists such as Alberto Giacometti and Joan Miró.

ABOVE The living room was defined by a long, low fireplace surround in rose-colored marble, a strong horizontal feature used by the architect in various configurations and materials in his interiors. The furniture, all designed by Marx in a straightforward, modern manner, recalled the work of Paris designer Jean-Michel Frank but was adapted by Marx to suit his own decidedly American standards of comfort and practicality. The two lounge chairs, upholstered in a densely textured tweed by Dorothy Liebes, provided a counterpoint to the hard surface of the mantelpiece. The silver and Lucite wall sconces in the form of stylized steer heads were designed by Haines.

ABOVE The first important modern painting purchased by the Marxes that set the standard for the future of their superb collection was Braque's 1935 *Yellow Tablecloth*. Centered in a trapezoid-shaped slice of bright yellow with tones of blue, beige, brown, and gray, the painting's dynamic composition achieves a sense of classical harmony by balancing color and form, structure, and surface decoration. Marx's Beaux-Arts training as an architect enabled him to recognize these merits even in the newly emerging style of the School of Paris artists that many of his generation found shocking. In 1965, Alfred H. Barr, Jr. noted "what gives the Marx collection its character is the dozen or so magnificent paintings that even ten years ago would have seemed, to most collectors, too big, too aggressive and too strong to live with."

LEFT Picasso's 1906 *Woman Plaiting Her Hair,* a masterpiece from his rose period, was acquired in 1939. It was one of several works in the collection formerly owned by the pioneering American collector John Quinn.

OPPOSITE In the library, the Picasso hung over the fossil stone mantelpiece. Marx covered the walls and ceiling in flexwood to create a subdued sense of chic, with plaid-patterned curtains continuing the soft, tonal palette. The lush shag, as well as the other hand-tufted carpets throughout the apartment, were made to order by Stanislav V'Soske at his workshops in Grand Rapids, Michigan. The innovative design of the armchair in the foreground, with its cantilevered back, was executed in burl wood, nickel, and patent leather.

ABOVE Marx was keenly aware of the work of his contemporaries and sometimes reinterpreted their more successful furniture designs to suit his own purposes, often upgrading and refining materials, finishes, and joinery. This lounge chair, executed by William J.Quigley, Inc. in limed oak with cotton webbing and upholstered cushions, recalls a similar design by the British-born T. H. Robsjohn-Gibbings.

RIGHT The living room, as it looked in 1957, illustrates the evolution of the room to accommodate the Marxes' growing art collection, which included Picasso's 1915 *Guitar over Fireplace* and his African-inspired *Bust of a Man* of 1908. The large display case, finished in crackle lacquer with Lucite handles, displayed fine Chinese ceramics against a background of shimmering gold leaf.

LEFT The Marxes were photographed at home for *Life* in 1952. A sense of ease and no-nonsense practicality belies the museum-quality works on view in their living room. Although pains were taken to refine each detail of the apartment's interiors, there is nothing fussy or precious about them. Picasso's surrealist *Head* of 1927, and the Miró ceramic vase executed by master ceramist Llorens Artigas at his studio in Gallifa, Spain, were later donated to the Art Institute of Chicago. Amedeo Modigliani's *Flower Vendor* of 1919 is now in the collection of the Metropolitan Museum of Art, in New York. In the corner stood a 1942 tall driftwood sculpture by Isamu Noguchi titled *My Pacific (Polynesian Culture)*.

ABOVE Many of Marx's furniture designs, like this three-tier bookcase in limed oak, were wonderfully simple and straightforward in design. Beautifully proportioned and finished in a muted tone, the bookcase served its purpose while adding a subtle sense of refinement.

ABOVE The large Matisse painting, *Variation on a Still Life by de Heem*, also known as *La Desserte*, of 1915, was purchased at auction for the Marxes in 1940 by his art dealer son, Pierre. This seminal work from one of the artist's most fruitful periods exhibits the rigorous structure and complex compositional elements Marx looked for in great works of art. The subject matter, which pays homage to the seventeenth-century Dutch master Jan Davidsz de Heem, would certainly have appealed to the architect, as it revealed the relationship of Matisse's modern work to the old-master tradition.

RIGHT AND BELOW RIGHT The architect covered the simple, rectilinear form of the Parsons-style dining table in malachite-green decorative paper, giving it added verve. The unusual ceiling fixture, designed by Marx, cast an ambient glow on the room and lit the chunky Lucite cubes suspending it. Two silver leaf folding screens stood by the serving table, whose recessed demilune base echoed the form of the ceiling light. The wall-mounted cabinet, in crackle lacquer with mirrored panels, added sparkle. In a nod to one of his contemporaries, Marx chose a chair by Donald Deskey, produced by the Royal Metal Manufacturing Company of Chicago, and made it his own by replacing the original perforated metal seat and back with deeply-tufted upholstery.

ABOVE In 1957, the library attested to the range and erudition of the Marxes' taste nearly twenty years after they made their first significant purchase. As the collection evolved, works were shifted from room to room as dictated by space but also to illuminate the intriguing relationships among various works. Roger de La Fresnaye's *Artillery* of 1911, with its kinetic composition and futuristic treatment of movement, related to the Bakota African sculptures, as well as to the round table that Marx designed in 1939.

OPPOSITE The leather-wrapped coffee table, with its glass top and propeller-like arrangement of shelves, demonstrated the extraordinary work Marx was able to produce through his unique association with Quigley, the expert Chicago cabinetmaker.

ABOVE *The Moroccans* of 1916, a spectacular early work by Matisse, was the crowning glory of the Marx collection. Purchased from the artist in 1951, the dynamic open-air scene set on a deep black ground promptly found pride of place in the living room, where the six-by-nine-foot canvas nearly touched the ceiling. With its vertical slab of bright pink and sensuous, rounded forms in green and golden yellow, the painting conjures up the artist's cherished visits to North Africa in a feat of temporal magic, and vividly demonstrates the clarifying power of memory in art. Identified by James Thrall Soby as "surely one of the greatest paintings of our time," it was the pièce de résistance of the historic 1965 School of Paris exhibition of the Marx collection at the Museum of Modern Art in New York.

ABOVE Pre-Columbian terracotta figures stood on either side of the large-scaled canvas. Marx used small Lucite tables, which he had made for himself and his clients by a local industrial plastics manufacturer, for their see-through appearance and practicality.

OPPOSITE Edgar Miller was commissioned by Marx to produce the beehive-shaped lamp bases in painted plaster. The pictorial scenes, sculpted in relief, depict a man on horseback setting out on a journey and, on the reverse, a female figure in an arched doorway awaiting his return. The architect used this model, usually made in white plaster, in many residential applications.

ABOVE Giorgio de Chirico's *Ariadne* of 1913 hung over the sofa in the sitting room. The painting, featuring a draped classical figure set slightly on the diagonal alongside the shadow of an arcaded passageway and with an enigmatic tower beyond, was the only example of this artist's work acquired by the Marxes. The sinuous form of the low table is similar to one by American furniture designer Harvey Probber.

LEFT AND OPPOSITE Many of Marx's furniture designs explore variations on a theme. In the library, a chest, left, has leather-faced drawers that are hand-tooled in imitation of book bindings and pillow out to serve as handles. In a sitting room, opposite, top right, the elegant simplicity of a writing table with a single drawer demonstrates the refined vision of Marx's furniture designs and the fine craftsmanship of the Quigley workrooms. The wall-mounted bookcase with its Greek key brackets and Lucite shelves is a variation of similar models the architect designed for special commissions. A chest of drawers, opposite, top left, in burl wood with a limed finish, has a strong rectilinear form, softened by subtle surface decoration. The wastepaper basket in burled elm with a chamfered base is a typical Marx design. A similar chest design, opposite, bottom left, finished in crackle lacquer has Lucite handles. The female heads in bisque are by French designer Colette Gueden, creative director of Primavera, the Paris store, and were probably purchased on one of the architect's trips abroad. A lady's dressing table, opposite, bottom right, in a more traditional style is paired with a wall cabinet of complementary design. Murano glass figurines and delightful table lamps add to the charm of the room.

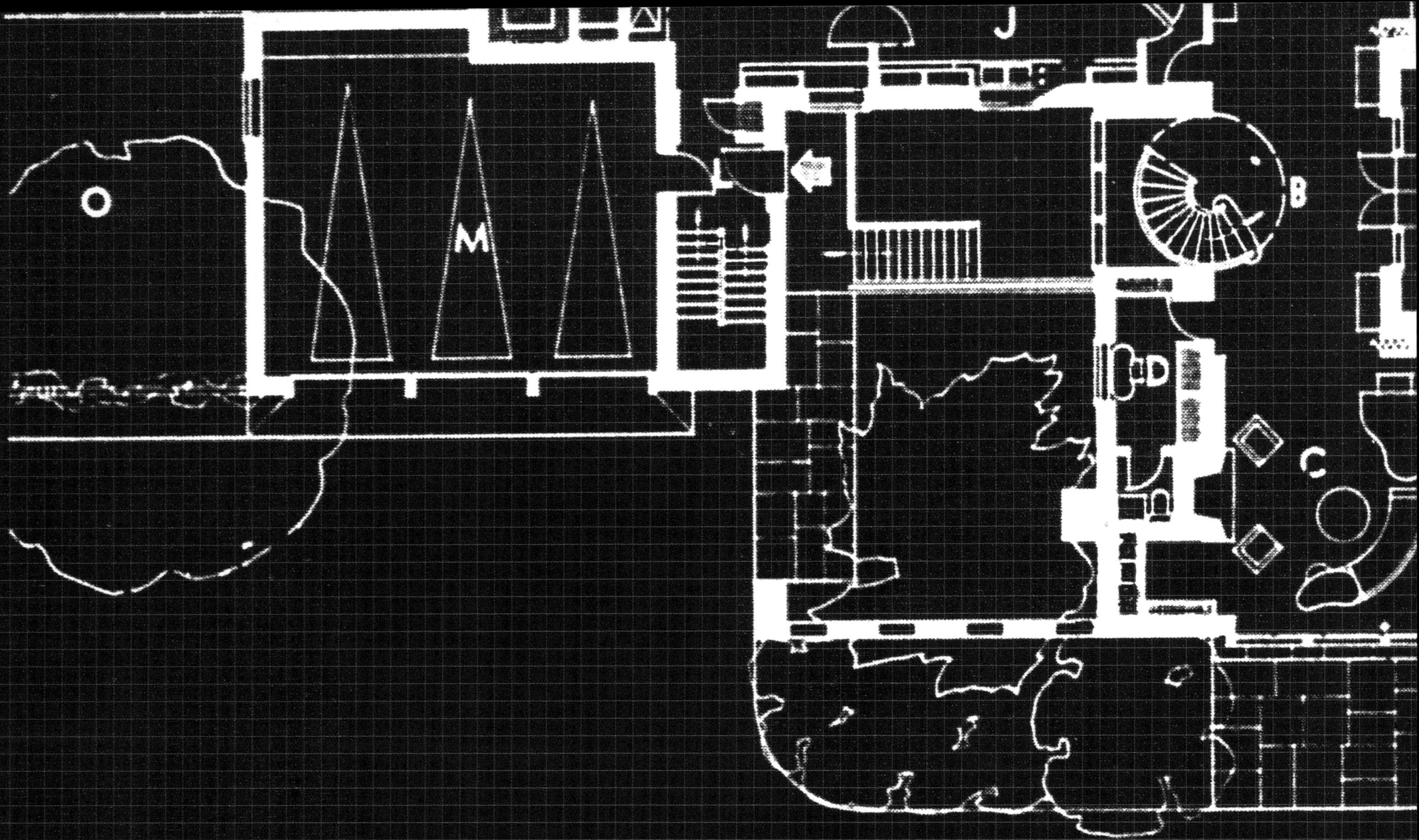

Throughout his marriage to Florene May, Marx undertook several commissions for the May family, including a number of innovative department stores in Los Angeles and St. Louis, as well as sleek, modern houses for Morton D. May in Ladue, Missouri, and Tom May in Los Angeles, California. Marx's bold designs for the May Company stores perfectly suited the changing patterns of retail shopping at the time—a shift from the main downtown stores to more suburban, automobile-friendly locations. Marx produced up-to-the-minute, multilevel buildings with sweeping curves and eye-catching signage that quickly became emblems of the May Company brand. With his daring applications of industrial materials, swank salons, cheeky murals, and stylish restaurants, Marx's sophisticated sense of style infused the design of the stores, which sold everything from evening gowns to garden furniture.

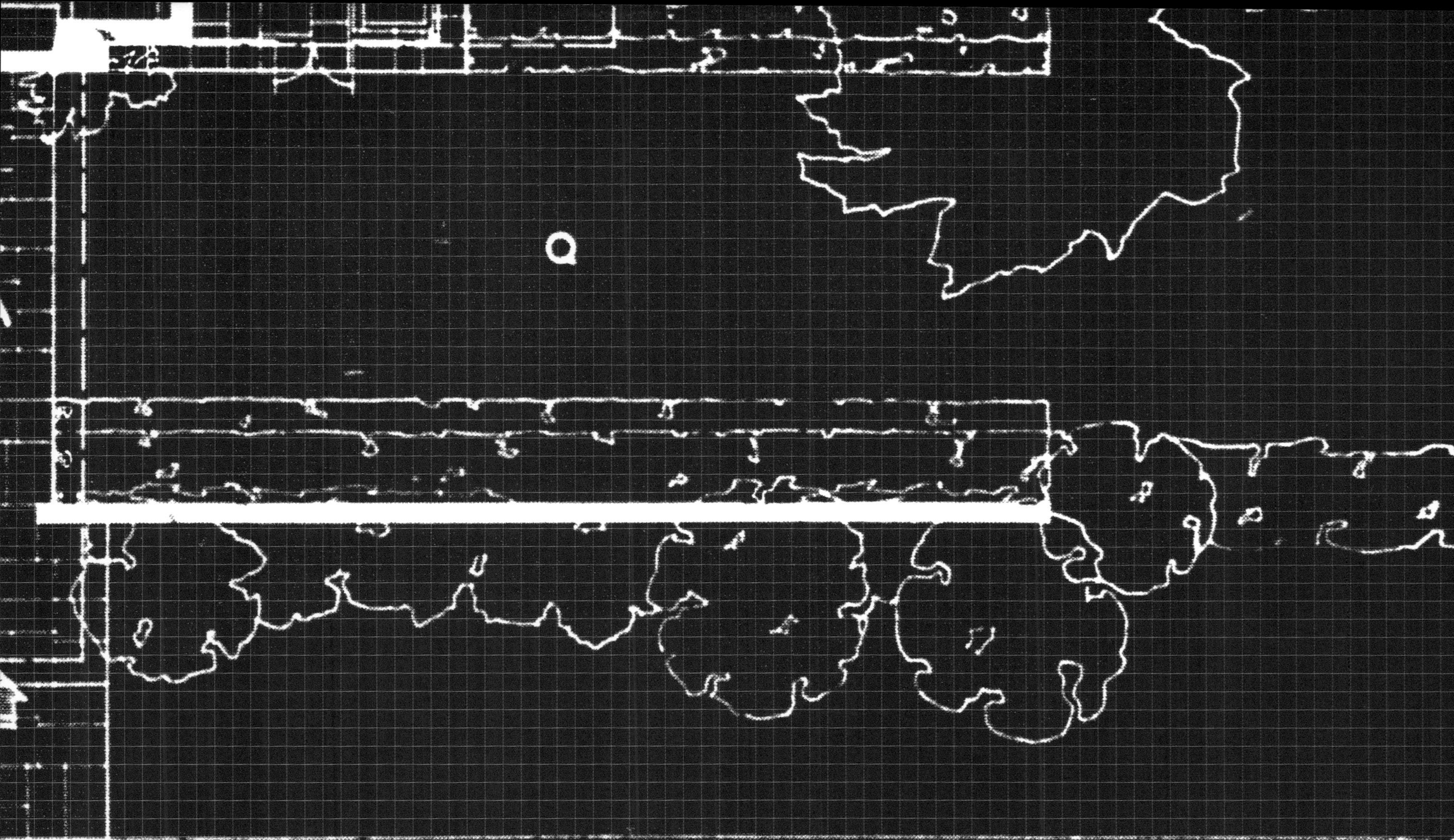

CHAPTER FOUR

ALL IN THE MAY FAMILY

PROJECT

Floor plan of Morton D. May house, Ladue, Missouri.

SAMUEL A. MARX • NOEL L. FLINT • CHARLES W. SCHONNE
ARCHITECTS
333 NORTH MICHIGAN • CHICAGO, ILLINOIS

DATE	REVISED	JOB	DRAWING
1940		Morton D. May	

In 1940, Marx designed a modern steel-frame house, elegant in construction and with an economy of decoration, for Florene's nephew Morton D. May in the affluent suburb of Ladue, Missouri. May, known to his friends as Buster, was the third member of the May family to serve as chairman of the St. Louis–based company. The International Style, flat-roofed house, with its asymmetrical massing and broad expanses of glass, stood apart from the Georgian and Colonial style houses in the bucolic, Midwestern community and signaled a new direction in residential work for the architect. With carte blanche from the twenty-six-year-old May, Marx was able to pursue his ideal of producing a harmonious, complete work of art, seamlessly integrating the building's architecture with its site, landscaping, and interiors. Set on a clearing with little shade, the house was one of the first private residences to feature central air-conditioning, which was installed at great expense. Marx also equipped the house with a darkroom for May, whose favorite hobby was photography. May credited Marx with introducing him to the pre-Columbian sculpture that became a lifelong obsession of the young merchant prince. Upon his death in 1983, May left a staggering number of primitive and modern works to the Saint Louis Art Museum, significantly enhancing the museum's holdings with a single, grand philanthropic gesture. In 2005, despite strenuous efforts by scholars, preservationists, and local residents, the house was razed to make way for new development.

PREVIOUS PAGES The large, two-story house sat serenely on a gently contoured nine-acre site. The building's façade, made of reclaimed brick, limestone, and concrete, produced surfaces varied in texture and material but unified in form and color.

ABOVE The back of the house, with its vast expanse of floor-to-ceiling windows, shaded by a long arc-shaped awning of cadmium yellow, hinted at the open, light-filled feel of the main living areas. A continuous ribbon of windows wrapped around the corners of the second floor, emphasizing the broad elevation.

ABOVE Chicago landscape designer Franz Lipp provided the minimalist plan for the grounds. The walled garden, set on axis to the front entrance but perpendicular to the approach of the house, allowed for privacy as well as access to the adjacent swimming pool. Lipp's design complemented the house beautifully, alternating screened passageways with enclosed areas, framed vistas, and open expanses of manicured lawn.

LEFT The helical staircase, sculpted in the round like a twisting ribbon in the shape of a giant conch shell, provided a graceful and dramatic counterpoint to the house's largely rectilinear plan. Marx drew inspiration from the freestanding, or flying, staircase he knew from childhood visits to Auburn, the antebellum mansion in Natchez, producing a modern, more muscular interpretation of the technical feat. The modern version also recalls Emilio Terry's project for a spiral form tower that had been exhibited in 1936 in New York at the Museum of Modern Art's exhibition, Fantastic Art, Dada, and Surrealism.

OPPOSITE The double-height entry hall led to an intriguing sequence of rooms ordered around the staircase. A tall vertical window, comprised of a grid of square panes, was framed by Dorothy Liebes curtains that puddled on the floor in neat folds. Marx designed the low slipper chair and table, which the Chicago cabinetmaker William J. Quigley executed.

ABOVE AND OPPOSITE Marx used glass curtain walls to create an airy sense of volume in the ground-floor living areas that blended seamlessly with the outdoors. A free-form sofa upholstered in a plush Liebes fabric and folding partitions divided the 2,300-square-foot floor into three separate living areas. The dining table's rectilinear form, enhanced by an exotic burl wood veneer, was paired with the same metal-framed dining chairs Marx used in his Chicago residence. Pulled up to a square card table were four chairs with webbing made of an early translucent resin called Vinylite, designed by Morris Sanders and produced by the B. L. Marble Chair Company of Bedford, Ohio. The lounge chairs, the low tables faced in glazed cork, and the round coffee table, opposite, were also by Marx.

MAY CO

MAY.CO

As part of the development of Wilshire Boulevard's Miracle Mile, a newly emerging shopping district halfway between downtown and Beverly Hills, the May Company store, with its ultramodern, streamlined design, became an instantly recognizable Los Angeles landmark when it opened in 1939. Marx, along with Los Angeles-based architect Albert C. Martin, produced a flat-roofed structure faced in black granite and limestone with a continuous band of street-level display windows shaded by a dramatically overhanging canopy. The sweeping curves of the corner site and elegant art moderne typeface recall architect Eric Mendelsohn's 1928 iconic avant-garde design for the Schocken store in Stuttgart, Germany, without seeking to duplicate its structural elegance. The cosmopolitan architecture elevated the prestige of the May Company, giving the mid-level retailer an air of glamour and sophistication. While the store was set flush to the street, as if to capture pedestrian traffic, the real hub of the store was its large 450-car parking lot in the rear. One customer remembers that a company employee was stationed on the roof of the building to direct shoppers to open parking spaces using a loud speaker. The Los Angeles County Museum of Art, which opened in 1965 on property adjacent to the May Company, purchased the building in 1991 and renamed it LACMA West.

PREVIOUS PAGES The four-story building, at the corner of Wilshire and Fairfax, with its curved corner of gleaming gold mosaic tiles, protruding signage, and distinctive fenestration, was designed to be easily visible to passing automobile traffic.

ABOVE LEFT Surfaces of steel, glass, and polished marble produced an aura of modern luxury in the intimate, boutique-like salons Marx created within the large structure.

LEFT The Tea Room, with its baroque chandeliers, sculpted mantelpiece, and striped, high-contrast window treatments brought Marx's signature supper club elements to a broad audience on the West Coast.

OPPOSITE The main floor of the 270,000-square-foot store was outfitted with sleek, illuminated display cases arranged around cylindrical columns. The open, high-ceilinged space, free of decorative detail, was designed to feature merchandise to its best advantage.

MAY·CO
MAY·CO

Seven years after opening the successful Wilshire Boulevard store, the May Company continued its expansion with a second Los Angeles location on Crenshaw Boulevard in the southwest section of the city. Marx, working again with Albert C. Martin, produced a variation on the earlier building, retaining key elements of design and signage that came to represent, in part, the company's identity. In an article describing it as "a department store Mecca for motorists," *Architectural Forum* called attention to the additional signage at the rear of the building and the orientation of the store's main entrance to the parking lot.

LEFT Built as a simple mass of reinforced concrete conforming to its irregular, wedge-shaped site, the Crenshaw location emerged as a pared-down version of its crosstown sister store. The distinctive corner treatment of four stacked bands separated by recessed openings gave the impression of a large ocean liner and added to the building's dramatic presence.

TOP AND ABOVE A preliminary rendering shows how the building would look at night with its backlit window displays and gleaming surfaces. The three bands of windows in the early design were revised in favor of one single, continuous ribbon wrapping around the whole structure.

OPPOSITE The storefront windows gave a partial view of the merchandise on display and brought natural light into the ground floor area.

RIGHT Indirect lighting provided a flattering glow in the millinery boutique, where shoppers could sit comfortably in individual niches to try on hats in front of a mirrored wall.

BELOW RIGHT Men's clothing and shoes were showcased in a masculine, club-like setting with wood paneled walls and chairs upholstered in faux leather.

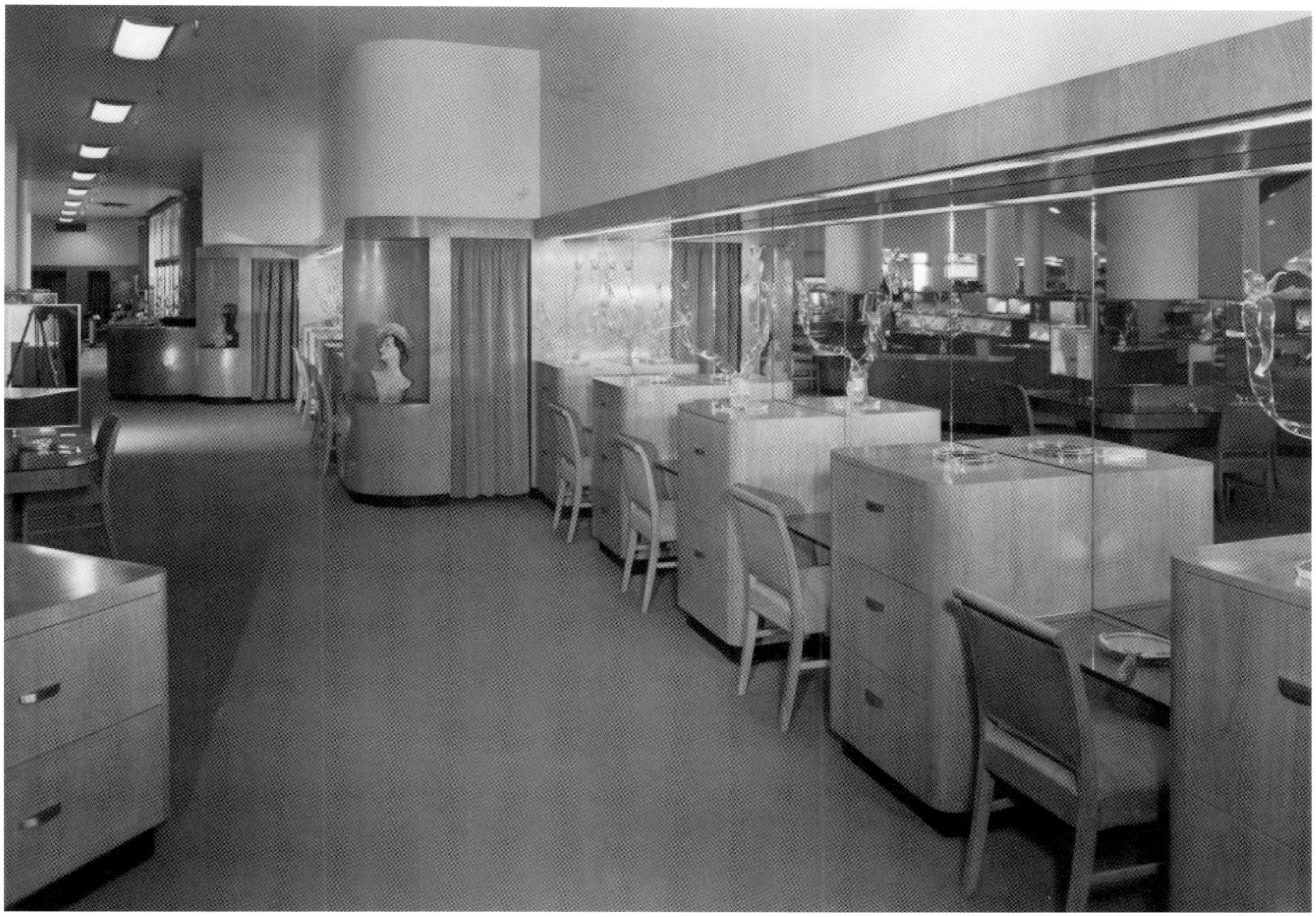

Of the Famous Barr stores Marx designed for the May Company around St. Louis, the one in the city of Clayton was by far the most memorable. Offering a mix of high-end fashion and everyday staples, "Clayton Famous," as it was known, was Morton May's own theatre of merchandising magic. Under the direction of general manager Stanley Goodman, news-making events like cooking demonstrations with Julia Child, appearances by European designers, and art exhibits selected by May made the store a glamorous, high-profile destination. As single-store locations gave way to the next wave in retail, Famous Barr, like the May stores in Los Angeles, was obliged to adapt to a new, multi-store shopping mall paradigm. In 1991, Famous Barr relocated to the Saint Louis Galleria just two miles west; Washington University eventually purchased the historic Clayton building, ensuring its preservation.

LEFT A rendering prepared by the St. Louis firm of Mauran, Russell, Crowell & Mullgardt appeared in local papers to publicize the 1948 opening of what May called, with true promotional élan, "the most modern, most beautiful store you've ever seen."

LEFT Marx designed an organic, free-form building of beige brick and black granite for the heavily trafficked Forsyth Boulevard site. A series of unusual square-shaped windows distinguished the façade, making a bold statement of individuality. Marx's interiors of the three-story structure further accentuated the forward style; several departments featured murals by Edgar Miller, including a humorous "birds and bees" theme in the maternity section. The upscale Wedgwood Room was a favorite spot for lunch, which locals remember with the same fond nostalgia customers feel in Dallas for Neiman Marcus' Zodiac Room and Chicago's Walnut Room at Marshall Field's.

OPPOSITE The 850-car parking lot, triple in size to the store's own footprint, was an indication of postwar shopping trends in America.

In 1952, Marx designed a house in the Holmby Hills section of Los Angeles for one of his wife Florene's three brothers, Tom May. At sixty-seven years of age, Marx's architectural career was in full form. With the complete confidence of his client, he was able to create a refined sense of spatial grandeur with a few bold and decisive gestures. Hollywood designer William Haines furnished the interiors of the 10,000-square-foot house; their collaboration produced a beautifully integrated whole of impressive luxury and refinement.

OPPOSITE The swimming pool, set parallel to the house but out of view of the main living areas, linked the main house to the cabana. The surface of the water acted as a reflecting pool, an effect that was especially dramatic when the house was lit at night.

ABOVE The upper level of the two-story residence was cantilevered over the windowed façade of the rear elevation, providing shade as well as visual appeal. The masterful treatment of this daring form created a sense of monumentality while simultaneously making the second floor appear to float.

LEFT The entry hall was defined by a highly original staircase enclosed by panels of clear glass attached with bronze mounts and topped with a leather-clad banister. The graceful curve of the second floor gallery drew the eye upward into the double-height space and accentuated the horizontal layout of the adjoining living room.

OPPOSITE The stairway landing was set squarely over the front door and backed by a series of windows. Ebonized wood floors, a few carefully chosen antiques, and Asian works of art gave a pleasing sense of contrast and clarity to the space awash in natural light.

ABOVE In the living room, Marx placed long, low shelves of fossil stone, a material he returned to again and again for its tawny beige tone and textured surface, on either side of the fireplace. The rectilinear treatment of this architectural feature provided a strong visual statement and related the interior to the façade of the house.

ABOVE A pair of recessed bookcases flanked the fireplace in the blue and white sitting area of Anita May's bedroom. Haines' original furniture designs complemented the architecture, with chic leather-wrapped tables, comfortable seating areas and groupings of fine art objects.

OVERLEAF The use of stainless steel, Formica, and enameled metal cabinets contributed to the forward design of the oversized kitchen. The extensive storage space and work surfaces reflected the Mays' custom of entertaining on a grand scale. A large live-in staff kept the household running smoothly.

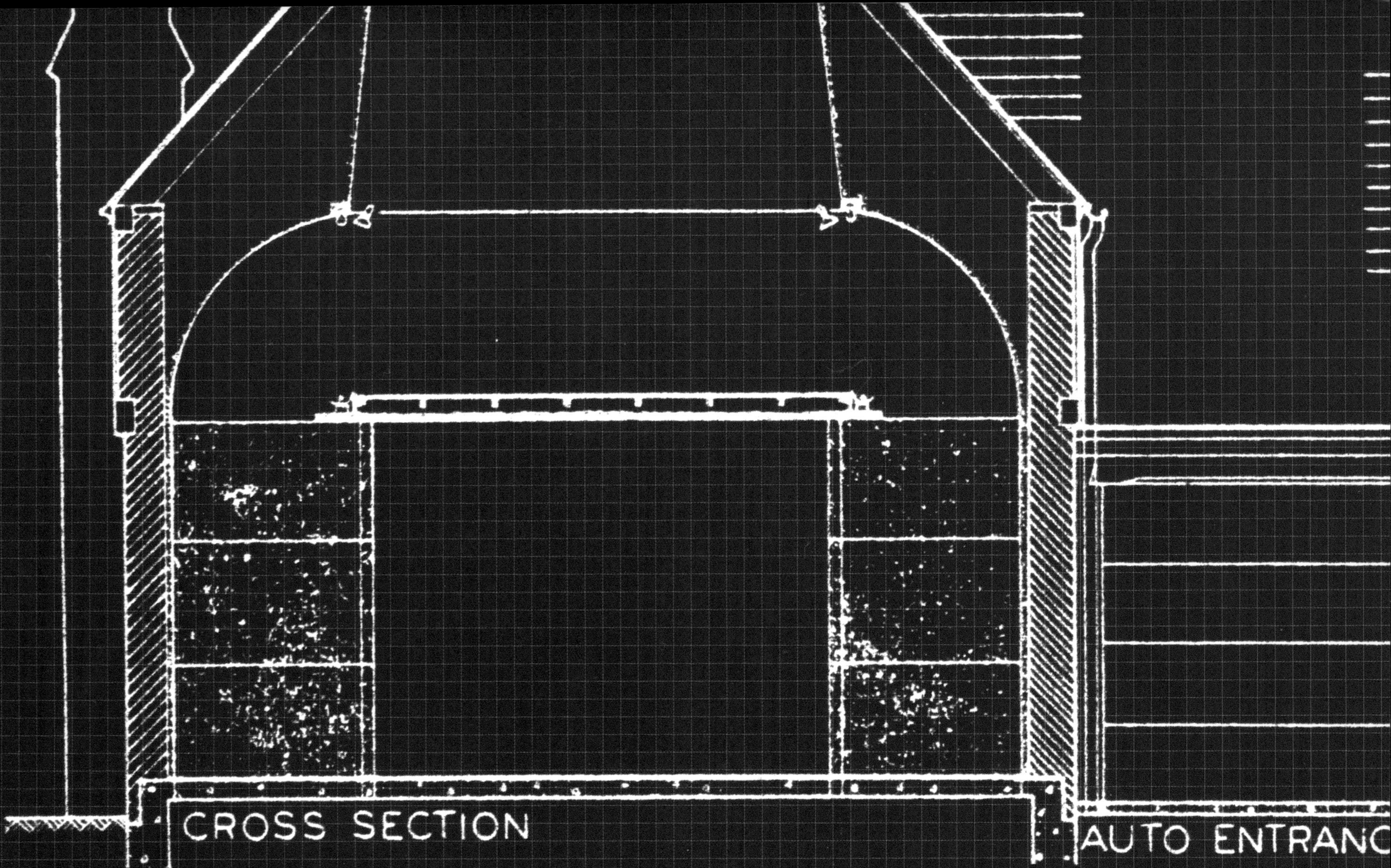

The Marxes, who were married in Los Angeles at the home of Florene's brother Wilbur May, traveled to the West Coast each winter visiting family and settling in for the season in Palm Springs, where they often stayed at a house William Haines had there. Marx conducted business from their desert address, communicating frequently with his Chicago office and, of course, art dealers and friends. In the 1940s and 1950s, Marx took on several residential commissions in Los Angeles, including work for Edward G. Robinson, Alfred Koolish, and Mervyn LeRoy. Robinson came to know Marx through New York art dealer Pierre Matisse and hired him to transform his Beverly Hills house and design a private art gallery on the property. Koolish, a Chicago businessman who had relocated to the area seeking to break into the movie business, sought out Marx to expand and remodel his Spanish style house in Bel Air. For LeRoy, the famed movie producer and director, Marx designed a modern house, also in Bel Air, worthy of Hollywood royalty.

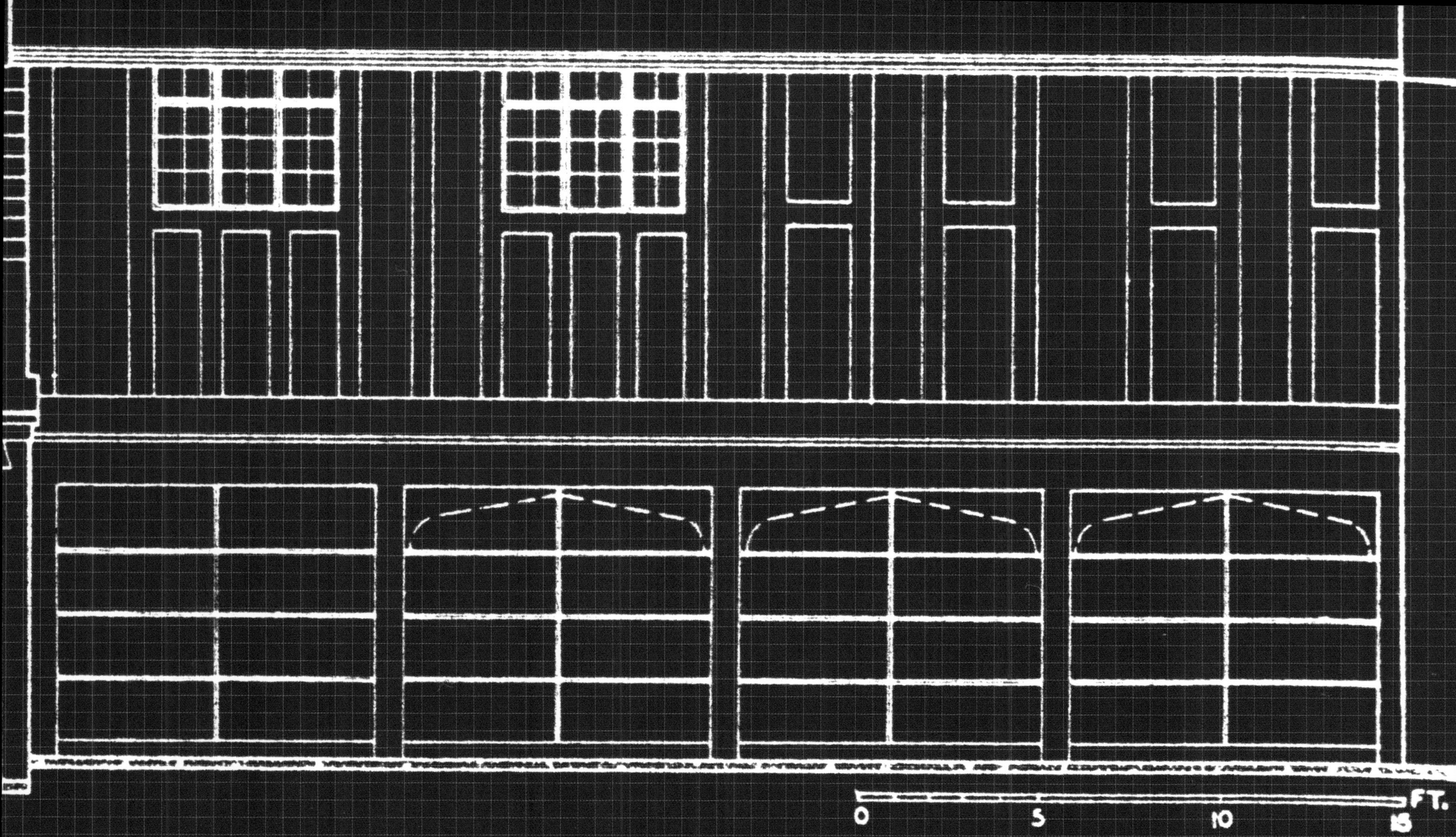

CHAPTER FIVE

WEST COAST CONNECTIONS

PROJECT

Elevation for art gallery, 910 North Rexford Drive, Beverly Hills.

SAMUEL A. MARX • NOEL L. FLINT • CHARLES W. SCHONNE

ARCHITECTS

333 NORTH MICHIGAN • CHICAGO, ILLINOIS

DATE	REVISED	JOB	DRAWING
1941		Edward G. Robinson	

ABOVE The entry hall of the Beverly Hills house featured a Marx staircase that wrapped around the second level, forming a gallery with ample space to hang several of Robinson's prized paintings by Pierre Bonnard, Edgar Degas, and Camille Pissarro. The gutsy scale of the doublewide doorframe, edged with a crown molding and topped with a broken pediment, showed Marx's assertive use of classical styles to make a fresh, modern statement. The painting of the Robinson family above the Chippendale-style chair was done by Edouard Vuillard in the actor's suite at the Hotel Plaza Athénée during a visit to Paris in 1939.

Early in 1941, Pierre Matisse arranged for Florene and Samuel Marx to call on Edward G. Robinson, the Hollywood actor best known for his starring roles in *Little Caesar* and *The Last Gangster*, to see his famed collection of Impressionist paintings on one of their yearly winter trips to the West Coast. Around the same time, Robinson became convinced that his collection could not be shown to its full advantage at his existing residence, a Tudor-style house on North Rexford Drive in Los Angeles, and was thinking about moving. "Great pictures are tyrants," he declared with customary bluster, saying that his paintings, which included works by Vincent van Gogh, Paul Cézanne, and Degas, "looked uncomfortable, small, and degraded" in what he called the gingerbread of the house.

Marx persuaded him otherwise. Robinson visited Chicago where he saw the architect's apartment as well as Max Epstein's home in Winnetka, Illinois, which impressed him with its dignity and livability. The actor hired Marx to do a thorough remodeling. Marx and Robinson hit it off from the start. Their early meetings were marked by lively exchanges on subjects ranging from the Fauves to Frank Lloyd Wright and the theatre designs of Gordon Craig. In addition to sharing a keen interest in collecting, both were amateur painters. Robinson was impressed with Marx's work as an architect, describing him as "sensitive and gifted," but did not approve of his taste in art, finding his avant-garde choices "wild and radical."

Thirty years after the architect's work was completed, Robinson said he was proud to have lived in a "house graced by his talent." Robinson's second wife, Jane, pointed out that he loved the house so much he paid for it twice, referring to the actor's much publicized 1956 divorce from his first wife, Gladys Lloyd, an event that forced him to sell his beloved art collection. An emotionally wrenching experience for Robinson, the sale of more than fifty-eight works to the Greek shipping tycoon Stavros Niarchos made national headlines.

RIGHT Robinson was photographed at home in 1964, after he was able to buy back a few of his paintings from Niarchos, such as Pablo Picasso's 1901 *Entombment*. In spite of trying for many years, he never succeeded in reclaiming the rest of his lost treasures.

LEFT The door frame, enriched with egg-and-dart and leaf-and-tongue decorations, opened onto the dining room where Jean-Baptiste-Camille Corot's *The Italian Woman* hung over the serving table, and silvered Chinese wall-paper, the height of fashion at the time, provided a rich and delightful backdrop for the Robinsons' frequent dinner parties. "If you think of movie stars in terms of wild parties around a swimming pool, don't come to our house," cautioned Jane Robinson, speaking of the couple's more civic-minded interests. The couple played host to a constant stream of actors, writers, politicians, and art connoisseurs, as well as world-famous musicians such as Arturo Toscanini, Vladimir Horowitz, and Sergei Prokofiev, all of whom obliged in signing the inside of the couple's piano after playing it.

ABOVE A portrait by Pierre-Auguste Renoir was set like a gemstone in the intricately carved overmantel in the living room. Chippendale chairs and candle stands in warm wood tones punctuated the neutral scheme used to highlight paintings such as Van Gogh's 1888 *Le Père Tanguy*. Interior designer Frances Elkins, who had made her home in Monterey, California, years earlier, was hired to furnish the rooms of the newly remodeled house. Her decor hit just the right note with a chic mix of period styles that suited the architecture, as well as the paintings, with elegant restraint.

OPPOSITE AND ABOVE As the remodeling progressed, architect and client both realized that more space was needed to accommodate the extensive range and number of Robinson's pictures. The solution, to build a free-standing, windowless art gallery adjacent to the main house, spoke directly to Marx's strengths. The gallery, made of fossil stone and plaster with dark brown cork floors, was built on the site formerly occupied by a badminton court and was joined to the main house with a porte cochère. The oblong-shaped approximately 2,000-square-foot space featured four protruding, fin-like panels that supported a dropped ceiling while also providing additional wall space. Above, skylights set into a pitched roof let in natural light, an ingenious solution for a space devoid of windows. At night, a system of recessed lights provided a dramatic, evenly distributed wash of light. A favorite painting of Robinson's, Matisse's 1897 *The Dinner Table*, was placed above one of Marx's trademark fireplaces. Sparse furnishings, large in scale but minimal in design, underscored the main purpose of the room, which displayed paintings by Claude Monet, Georges Rouault, and Maurice Utrillo. Continuous grooves built into the walls allowed for the art works to be easily rearranged.

In Los Angeles in the early fifties, Marx remodeled a 1920s Spanish-style villa in the hills of Bel Air for Chicago transplant Alfred Koolish. Marx retained much of the original structure, built as a series of terraced levels conforming to the slope of the hillside site, but altered the plan dramatically to produce open, light-filled spaces. Los Angeles landscape designer Garrett Eckbo planned the grounds in a naturalistic manner consistent with the wooded canyon setting. Marx custom-designed all the furniture, which was executed in Chicago by William J. Quigley.

LEFT AND ABOVE Raised walkways connected the main house to the garden, a separate pool area, and the new cabana added by Marx.

ABOVE A wood-framed door was set in the glass curtain wall that enclosed the entry hall and sunken dining room. The architect replaced the original load-bearing wall with a single slender column, in keeping with the new, open plan. A built-in well containing tropical plants merged the indoor space with the lush vegetation of the garden. The long, low bench in burl wood set along the glass partition accentuated the oblong thrust of the entry hall.

ABOVE Chairs upholstered in a Dorothy Liebes plaid chenille of slate gray, beige, and silver Lurex were placed around a black lacquer Parsons-style dining table.

LEFT Marx adapted a chair design by T.H. Robsjohn-Gibbings to his own specifications with a limed oak frame and nickel handle. The armrest, set a few inches below the usual elbow height, provided a surprisingly comfortable improvement on the original.

ABOVE The pair of andirons, in the form of two interlocking rectangles, were designed by Marx especially for the fireplace in the living room.

RIGHT The wood-beamed ceiling of the living room followed the pitch of the roof up to the third floor. Marx created a sense of volume by replacing the exterior wall with a continuous series of floor-to-ceiling glass panels, with a door at the corner that opened onto the garden. A four-door cabinet with block handles sectioned off the main living area. The Chinese rubbing of a prancing horse over the fireplace may well have been the same one that hung years earlier in the architect's Chicago apartment.

ABOVE The andiron design in the form of a stylized longhorn steer head in brushed nickel hinted at the room's Southwestern motif and recalled the wall sconces by William Haines that Marx had in his own apartment.

ABOVE The library, centered on a fossil stone fireplace surround, featured furniture in a variety of earthy materials—an oval coffee table of glazed cork, crackle glazed side tables, and a desk chair of woven leather. Pre-Columbian artifacts showed the influence of the designer's taste and erudition on the collecting habits of his clients.

The way to a man's heart
The Settlement

OPPOSITE AND RIGHT The L-shaped kitchen with its modern fixtures and black Formica counter tops was adapted to the unusual configuration of the house.

BOTTOM RIGHT A small table with four painted metal chairs was in the glass-enclosed corner niche.

Around 1948, Marx designed a posh, modern showplace for Kitty and Mervyn LeRoy in the Bel Air neighborhood of Los Angeles. The architect would have known the celebrated producer of *The Wizard of Oz* through any number of mutual acquaitances, including Edward G. Robinson. The actor had starred in LeRoy's 1930 gangster epic, *Little Caesar*, the hit that made both of their careers. But it was thanks to LeRoy's third wife, Kitty, a Chicagoan and ex-wife of hotelier Ernest Byfield, that Marx was commissioned to build their 11,000-square-foot house on St. Cloud Road.

RIGHT Shaded by a deep overhang, the wall of windows with sliding glass doors opening onto the garden and pool area recall the design of the Tom May house, which was built several years later. Custom-made furniture designed by Marx, including the two parchment lamp tables, the free-form coffee table, and the low slipper chairs, suited the large open plan of the living room. LeRoy's daughter, Linda Janklow, recalls the square card table and chairs as the scene of her father's weekend games of gin rummy with Hollywood friends such as Jack Benny, Walter O'Malley, and Jules Stein. The house was later owned by television talk show host Johnny Carson, who purchased it from the LeRoys in 1972 when *The Tonight Show* moved from New York to the West Coast.

ABOVE The easy, open arrangement of furniture offered ample seating and set the stage for the LeRoys frequent entertaining. Folding partitions were designed to close off the living room, which doubled as a private screening room for small gatherings of family and friends.

RIGHT Marx frequently chose ancient Chinese ceramics for their sculptural quality and decorative appeal. C.T. Loo, the Paris dealer who exhibited regularly at the Arts Club of Chicago, and Ralph M. Chait Galleries in New York, were favorite sources of the architect and his clients.

LEFT Kappa shell—a Marx trademark—covered the walls of the dining room, which gave the room a soft opalescent luster. Smoked mirror was used for the front of the clapboard serving cabinet and the faceted frame of the wall mirror that was based on an eighteenth-century Venetian model. A pair of Lucite standards supported the dining table's lacquered top. The chairs, adapted from an earlier design in metal, were executed by Quigley in cream-colored lacquer with a crackle glaze. A freestanding bamboo screen by Liebes stood in the corner.

ABOVE A film projector was cleverly concealed behind one of the LeRoys' modern pictures including, at center, a painting by Marx of a vase of flowers set on a chair the architect gave to the LeRoys as a gift.

Marx took on several residential commissions in Chicago for the socially prominent Block family, who headed the Inland Steel company for the better part of the twentieth century. Leopold Block served as chairman from 1919 through 1940. His two sons, Joseph and Leigh, along with their cousin, Philip D. Block, Jr., formed the leadership of the next generation, with Joseph serving as president starting in 1953 and becoming chairman in 1959. In the 1940s, Marx designed apartments for the two brothers, one for Joseph at 1325 North Astor Street, and one for Leigh down the block in the Philip B. Maher art moderne building at number 1260, famed address of other Chicago luminaries such as Potter Palmer III and Sterling Morton, of Morton Salt. Marx's work for the Blocks demonstrates the originality of his designs—one with a consistent vocabulary of form that lent itself to unlimited variation resulting in a style instantly recognizable as "Marx" while still reflecting the unique tastes and requirements of each client.

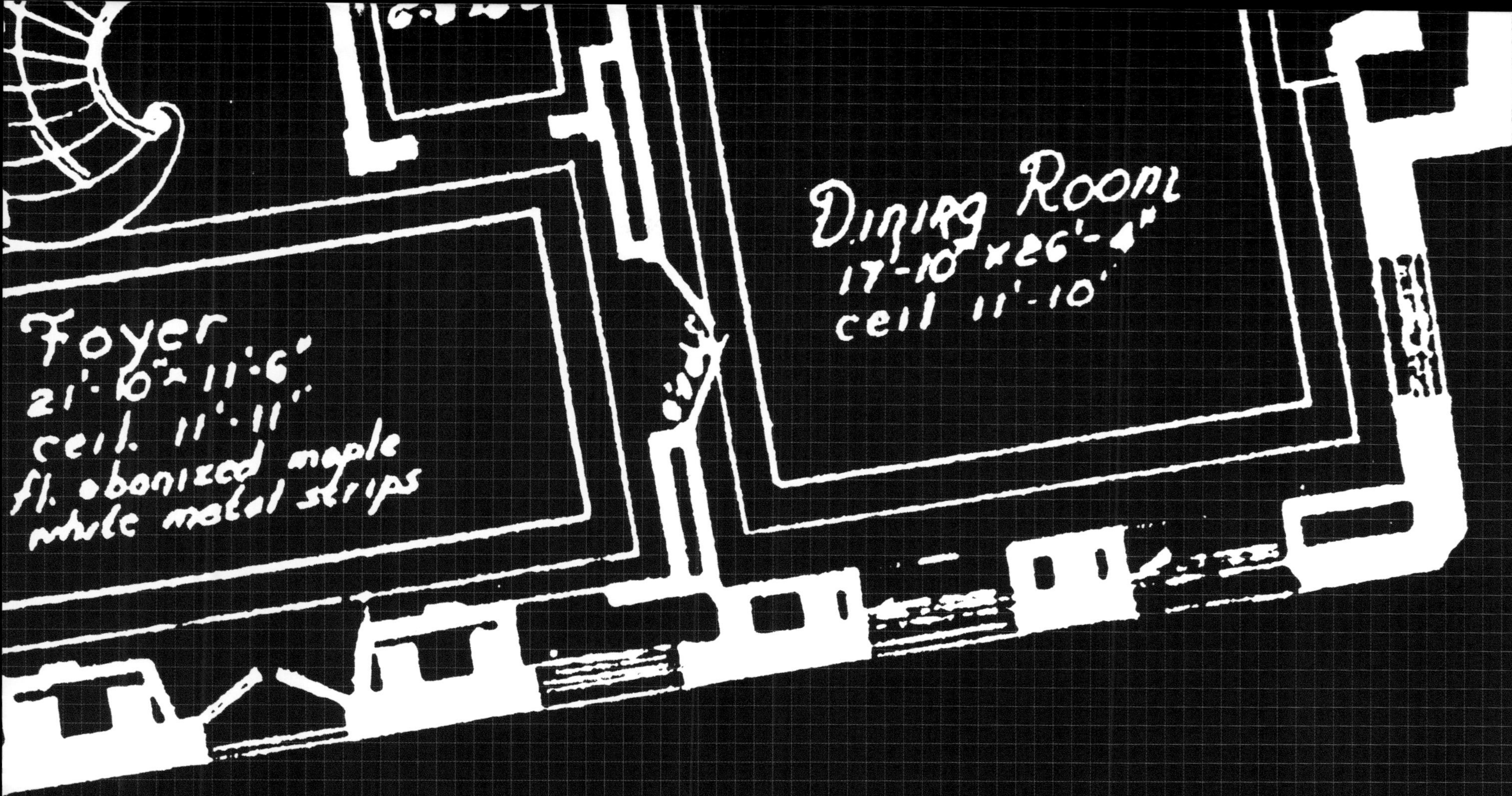

CHAPTER SIX

PERFECT PATRONS

PROJECT

Apartment, 1260 North Astor Street, Chicago.

SAMUEL A. MARX • NOEL L. FLINT • CHARLES W. SCHONNE

ARCHITECTS

333 NORTH MICHIGAN • CHICAGO, ILLINOIS

DATE	REVISED	JOB	DRAWING
1943		Leigh B. Block	

Shortly after Leigh B. Block married Mary Lasker Foreman, daughter of the legendary advertising pioneer Albert D. Lasker, in 1942, the two art connoisseurs began a collection of painting and sculpture soon regarded as one of the finest in the country. The couple, who had made their first purchase, a Georges Braque still life, while on their honeymoon, decided from the start that they had to be in complete agreement on each purchase. With their shared passion, they spent the next four decades amassing works by artists as varied as Jan Brueghel, Jean-Honoré Fragonard, and Fernand Léger.

If the Marxes' collection was exceptional for its focus and rigorous selectivity, the Blocks countered with a glorious array of jewel-like masterpieces whose vivid colors and rich sensual beauty enlivened room after room of their North Astor Street apartment.

The apartment Marx designed for the couple in 1943 featured many of his signature touches—stone fireplaces, distinctive wall finishes, luxurious hand-woven fabrics by Dorothy Liebes, and original furniture designs produced by William J. Quigley, Inc. in tonal shades of parchment and cream-colored lacquer. In keeping with his clients' tastes and preferences, Marx chose deeper colors and softer, less strictly rectilinear forms to produce gracious interiors that proved to be the perfect setting for their numerous acquisitions. Mary Block's statement that "We don't buy names" may seem incongruous vis-à-vis their collection of works by Vincent van Gogh, Paul Cézanne, and Edgar Degas, but it speaks to their commitment of evaluating each piece individually, as evidenced by the intimate, even nonchalant placement of the works throughout their home.

ABOVE A pair of unusually-shaped side tables in crackle lacquer have a raised round top on an open, cube-shaped base with gently serpentine sides. Marx used this favorite model in several of his commissions.

RIGHT Mary and Leigh Block were photographed in the living room of their North Astor Street apartment for *Life* in 1952 in an issue featuring Chicago collectors. Van Gogh's 1889 *Self Portrait with Bandaged Ear and a Pipe* hung in a grouping with Henri Rousseau's 1910 *Exotic Landscape* and Cézanne's 1906 *Portrait of the Gardener, Vallier*.

Mary and Leigh Block, opposite, were chief benefactors of the Art Institute of Chicago and played leadership roles at the august institution for many years. Leigh served as a trustee from 1949, and later as president and then chairman from 1970 to 1975. Mary was a founding member of the Women's Board and a long-standing trustee.

LEFT Picasso's *Still Life with Chair* of 1943 hung over a two-door cabinet of giltwood and mirror. A bronze by Jacques Lipchitz and a Braque ceramic plate were displayed in front of the painting.

OPPOSITE The apartment was furnished with a genial mix of modern forms and period styles finished in plush velvet, parchment, and silver leaf. The tonal scheme provided a sumptuous backdrop for works such as a large pastel by Degas.

ABOVE A leather-wrapped console table with a rectangular opening was designed to conform to the curved wall separating the living room from the entry hall. Matisse's *Two Musicians*, circa 1921, anchored a grouping of smaller works by Edouard Vuillard, Renoir, Cézanne, and Georges Seurat. Several standing figures by Marino Marini, arranged with ancient Chinese and Etruscan bronzes, attested to the Blocks' exquisite taste and broad range of connoisseurship.

LEFT The pedestal table in crackle lacquer with a triangular glass top was custom-designed for the apartment. Donated to the Art Institute of Chicago in 1981 when the Blocks moved to Santa Barbara, California, it has been on view for many years in the American Furniture galleries amid works by Louis Sullivan, Frank Lloyd Wright, and Charles Eames.

ABOVE Van Gogh's *Town Hall at Auvers*, painted in 1890 just two weeks before the artist committed suicide, and a painting by Chaim Soutine hung in the salon-like atmosphere of the library, which was remarkable for its deep rose-colored walls and loop-fringed drapes by Liebes.

OPPOSITE The dining room doubled as a gallery of Braque paintings with the artist's dynamic 1949 *Billiard Table*, purchased directly from the artist in 1950, as its centerpiece.

RIGHT The same dining room, shown on the cover of the March 1947 issue of *House Beautiful*, featured a painting by Raoul Dufy. The marbleized wall treatment in soft coppery tones extended to the surface of the serving cabinet Marx designed with a louvered front and a façade of smoked mirror.

OPPOSITE A daring arrangement of drawings by Degas, Léger, Picasso, Juan Gris, Amedeo Modigliani, and Seurat, installed edge to edge in the hallway near the master bedroom, made an effective decorative statement. Marx did not treat works of art as precious or imposing objects to be revered, but rather sought out intriguing relationships and was adept at creating environments in which his clients could do the same.

RIGHT The voluptuous form of Hans Arp's organic sculpture *Pyrenäen-Torso* was paired with Picasso's 1924 *Harlequin with Guitar* to produce a lively, if unexpected, juxtaposition.

ABOVE An L-shaped desk was designed in crackle lacquer for Mary Block's much-used study. African and pre-Columbian works such as a Punu mask from Gabon, an alabaster mask from Vera Cruz, and a Colima pottery figure decorated the tabletops. The bold placement of a 1912 cubist painting by Picasso directly over a door frame between Pierre Bonnard's *Green Slipper* and Picasso's 1962 *Head of a Woman* demonstrated the Blocks' overriding passion for the works they collected.

ABOVE A lineup of paintings by Gris and Picasso in a corner of the study presented an impromptu lesson in baroque cubism. A bronze standing figure by Alberto Giacometti vied for space on a Marx-designed table crowded with books, art objects by Matisse and Picasso, an Edgar Miller table lamp, and everyday items such as a telephone.

RIGHT A daring tableau of art and objects in Mary Block's study illustrated the couple's catholicity of taste. Picasso's 1938 *The Sailor* was hung with a 1911 Braque still life and Soutine's 1925 *French Cook*. Two open-backed side chairs upholstered in chic patent leather stood by a writing table topped with Toltec plates and pre-Columbian sculptures.

CENTER RIGHT Works by Cézanne and Van Gogh were displayed alongside Fragonard's circa 1770 *Portrait of a Man as Don Quixote* to highlight the influence of the eighteenth-century master on modern painting. A sofa upholstered in cream-colored damask and silver leaf tables recall the subtly opulent details Marx used in earlier commissions.

BOTTOM RIGHT Georges Rouault's *Passion* of 1912, with Vuillard's *Self-portrait* of 1893 and a Degas portrait of 1887, were positioned above a sofa upholstered in a cream and yellow-striped tweed. A small Matisse bronze is on one of a pair of Marx lacquered side tables.

OPPOSITE The generously proportioned three-tier side table with its square shape and concave sides and corners executed by Quigley in crackle lacquer, accommodated lamps and small objects, as well as books and magazines.

In 1946, Marx undertook the complete renovation of a large apartment at 1325 North Astor Street for Joseph L. Block and his family. Starting with the same floor plan as his own home in the same building, Marx took down walls to create large, open living areas and installed bold architectural elements with the big-shouldered appeal of Chicago itself. In contrast to the soft, tonal mood the architect had created for the Leigh Block apartment, where the art collection was the main visual focus, the Joseph Block residence featured a masculine, assertive design, which created a strong statement of its own.

ABOVE Block, his wife Lucille, and their daughter Susan relaxed in the wood paneled library. Mr. Block's collection of historical documents and Abraham Lincoln memorabilia was framed and installed into the boiserie. The fossil stone fireplace and cube-shaped andirons in brushed nickel lent a casual, earthy air to the room, to which Marx added leather-wrapped furniture and upholstery in a warm palette of yellow, beige, and orange.

OPPOSITE Two lounge chairs, ideal for reading, were covered in a hand-woven Liebes fabric shot through with metallic yarn. The round magazine table of dark walnut and glass was an original design Marx used in several commissions because of its practicality and dynamic appearance.

LEFT The rectilinear design of the low table took on a glamorous air with its shimmering surface of mirrored glass panels.

BELOW LEFT Another variation of the low table, paved in *verre églomisé*, or reverse painted glass, was made in emerald green, silver, and black. The upholstered seating was covered in a lively, outline-quilted floral chintz.

OPPOSITE The long, low profile of the green marble fireplace and the bold scale of the wall mirror with its faceted panels of smoky silvered glass gave the living room a sense of modern drama. The andirons, modeled after a design by Alberto Giacometti, were scaled up and finished in brushed nickel.

LEFT Marx finished the large custom bookcase in the same marbleized surface as the walls, with shades of green and putty gray.

OPPOSITE The walls and cabinets of the kitchen, with its machine-age table and chairs, were lined in gray Vitrolite, an opaque, structural glass product marketed by the Libby Owens Ford Glass Company of Toledo, Ohio.

ABOVE The walls of the guest room were sheathed in unadorned silver leaf. Two signature Marx chests in crackle lacquer with block handles flanked the parchment daybed overspread with printed linen. The coverlet's bold painterly graphic of doves and fruit trees reminiscent of period fabrics by designers such as Ruth Reeves, may well have been the work of Miller. Two Queen Anne–style armchairs, produced by Quigley in cream-colored lacquer, exemplify the cabinetmaker's virtuoso craftsmanship and Marx's deft reinterpretation of historical models for use in chic modern interiors.

ABOVE A view of Lucille Block at work in the sitting area of the master bedroom shows the extensive built-in cabinets of the adjoining dressing room. In city apartments and country houses alike, Marx designed carefully thought-out storage systems in spacious rooms detailed for maximum style and utility. Mrs. Block lived in the apartment for more than fifty years, keeping it intact until the time of her death in 2002.

OPPOSITE Dorothy Liebes, the grande dame of American textiles, parlayed a correspondence course in weaving into a stunningly successful career as a textile producer, educator, and industry spokesperson. Her personal style and good looks made her a favorite of magazine editors, who featured her, as well as her innovative fabrics, on countless magazine covers in the 1940s and 1950s. Liebes, a talented colorist who proclaimed, "There are no bad colors, just bad color combinations," was retained by firms such as Goodall and DuPont to bring her modern flair to their product development efforts in the postwar years. Marx, who, as early as 1939, was among the first architects to place custom orders with her Powell Street studio in San Francisco, used Liebes fabrics extensively in his interiors, usually specifying more tranquil color schemes of beige, off-white, slate gray, and soft yellows.

RIGHT The couture quality of these loop-fringe drapery panels epitomizes the soigné modern luxe of Liebes' work. Marx used similar fabrics, often shot through with silver or gold Lurex yarn, in commissions for Mary and Leigh Block and Morton D. May.

Marx's association with William J. Quigley, Inc. extended over several decades. Early on he would have turned to them for the quality reproductions they were known for. In the 1930s he had begun to develop his original modern designs that were ordered specifically for each commission. By the 1950s, he was single-handedly keeping them in business. In addition to relying on their workrooms to execute furniture, Marx ordered window treatments, upholstery, and custom picture framing. Estimates went on for pages, specifying materials and finishes down to the smallest detail.

At its peak, Quigley, who produced quality reproductions of English and American period furniture as well as Samuel Marx's own original modern designs, had several locations. The main site, at 117 East Delaware Place in Chicago, housed extensive workrooms where woodworking, upholstery, and window treatments were executed for Chicago's elite by a small army of skilled artisans. In an oral history for the Art Institute of Chicago, architect Ernest A. Grunsfeld III recalled visiting Quigley with his father, an architect who ordered custom furniture there: "They were very successful, very busy, and you'd have to wait months. You'd almost have to buy your furniture before you designed the house so it would arrive at the same time. It was easier to get a house built than a sofa," he said.

In 1948, *House Beautiful* predicted, "Time will probably prove that [Marx's] most influential contribution to furniture design is his persistent experimentation with finishes. He is intrigued by the decorative values of wood patinas that bring out the grains and textures of wood. In his famous crackle finish he has created a sort of hallmark." Marx opted for American materials such as oak and burled elm, enriching their surfaces with highly distinctive finishes. Unlike designers working in France at the time who were drawing on the rich resources of the French colonies, Marx didn't use precious or exotic materials such as shagreen, rosewood, or ivory inlay. His choice of local materials and his celebration of the skills of the country's artisans resulted in an original and authentically American style.

ABOVE LEFT A photograph shows the storefront of the William J. Quigley, Inc. Bank Street shop in Lake Forest, Illinois, as it appeared in a 1930 magazine.

100 European Paintings and Drawings from the Collection of Mr. and Mrs. Leigh B. Block. Washington, DC: National Gallery of Art, 1967.

Addade, Stéphane-Jacques. *Bernard Boutet de Monvel*. Paris: Les Éditions de l'Amateur, 2001.

"A Department Store Mecca for Motorists Built to Serve a Widespread Population." *Architectural Forum*, May 1948, 108–109.

"A New Impetus to Modern Design." *Interior Design & Decoration*, April 1941, 22–25.

"Architectural Alchemy Turns Unused Space into a Suspended Bar." *Interiors*, March 1957, 156–157.

Ascoli, Peter M. *Julius Rosenwald: The Man Who Built Sears, Roebuck and Advanced the Cause of Black Education in the American South*. Indiana: Indiana University Press, 2006.

Barr, Alfred H. Jr., ed. *Fantastic Art, Dada, Surrealism*. New York: The Museum of Modern Art, 1936.

Barr, Alfred H. Jr. and James Thrall Soby. *The School of Paris: Paintings from the Florene May Schoenborn and Samuel A Marx Collection*. New York: The Museum of Modern Art, 1965.

Berggruen, Heinz. *Highway and Byways*. Northamptonshire, England: Pilkington Press, 1998.

Bossom, Alfred, C. G. Holme and John Holme. *Decorative Art 1942: The Studio Yearbook*. London: The Studio, Ltd., 1942.

Cass, Judith. "Many Arrange Holiday Parties for Arts Club: Expect New Quarters to be Opened Soon." *Chicago Daily Tribune*, November 24, 1936.

———. "New Home of Arts Club Near Its Completion." *Chicago Daily Tribune*, September 20, 1936.

"Cellar Sgraffiti: An Ancient Process Brings New Murals by Edgar Miller to a Hotel Grill." *Interiors*, April 1946, 114–156.

Clarke, Gerald. "Mervyn LeRoy: The *Gone with the Wind* Producer's Contemporary House in Bel-Air." *Architectural Digest*, April 1994, 226–286.

Cohen, Stuart and Susan Benjamin. *North Shore Chicago: Houses of the Lakefront Suburbs 1890–1940*. New York: Acanthus Press, 2004.

"Connoisseur's Modern: S. A. Marx Apartment, Chicago." *House and Garden*, April 1941, 34–37.

"Contemporary Decoration." *Architect and Engineer*, March 1946, 23.

Cooper, Douglas, ed. *Great Private Collections*. New York: The Macmillan Company, 1963.

Darling, Sharon. *Chicago Furniture: Art, Craft, and Industry 1833–1983*. Chicago: Chicago Historical Society, 1984.

Davis, Deering. *Contemporary Décor: Restaurants, Lounges, Bars*. New York: Architectural Book Publishing Company, 1950.

Day, Susan. *Jean-Charles Moreux: Architecte-Décorateur-Paysagiste*. Paris: Norma Editions, 1999.

De Anno Tabernae 1957. Chicago: The Tavern Club of Chicago, 1958.

"Decorating the Business Office." *Good Furniture*, September 1928, 135.

Decorative Arts. Official catalog, Department of Fine Arts, Division of Decorative Arts, Golden Gate International Exposition, San Francisco, 1939.

"Delgado Art Corner Stone Laid Dedication on the Fourth of July." *Daily Picayune*, March 23, 1911.

"Delgado Art Museum Design Awarded to Chicago Firm." *Daily Picayune*, July 5, 1910.

"Delgado's Museum." *The Times Democrat*, December 10, 1911.

"Department Store for the May Department Stores Co., Los Angeles, California." *Architectural Forum*, May 1940, 353–357.

"Deposit for Art Gallery." *Daily States*, March 10, 1910.

Dorothy Liebes. Catalog of the retrospective exhibition sponsored by the Textile Fibers Department, E. I. DuPont De Nemours & Company. New York: Museum of Contemporary Craft, 1970.

"Dorothy Wright Liebes: Textile Designer." *Architect and Engineer*, March 1946, 25.

Drexler, Arthur, ed. *The Architecture of the Ecole des Beaux-Arts*. New York: The Museum of Modern Art, 1977.

Dunbar, Prescott N. *The New Orleans Museum of Art: The First Seventy-Five Years*. Louisiana: Louisiana State University Press, 1990.

Du Plessix, Francine. "Collectors: Mary and Leigh Block." *Art in America*, September/October 1966, 64–75.

Feigen, Richard. *Tales from the Art Crypt*. New York: Alfred A. Knopf, 2000.

Ford, James & Katherine Morrow Ford. *Design of Modern Interiors*. New York: Architectural Book Publishing Company, 1942.

Forty Paintings from the Edward G. Robinson Collection: March 4–April 12, 1953. New York: The Metropolitan Museum of Art, 1953.

Frank, Michael. "Edward G. Robinson: Sterling Collection for the Star of *Little Caesar* and *Double Indemnity*." *Architectural Digest*, April 1990, 180–183.

"Furniture That Starts as Architecture: Grounded in the Past...but Appreciative of the Future." *House Beautiful*, October 1948, 148–151, 210, 279.

Glueck, Grace. "A Surprise, and Then a Collection." *The New York Times*, February 28, 1997.

Gough, Marion. "How to Develop an Appreciation of Art." *House Beautiful*, March 1947, 78–82.

Halsey, R. T. H. and Elizabeth Tower. *The Homes of Our Ancestors*. New York: Doubleday, 1925.

Hanks, David A. with Jennifer Toher. *Donald Deskey: Decorative Designs and Interiors*. New York: E. P. Dutton, 1987.

Harris, Neil. *Chicago Apartments: A Century of Lakefront Luxury*. New York: Acanthus Press, 2004.

Hedlund, Marilou. "Tenants May Come and Go in Chicago Apartment Buildings, but Not in Two That the Late Andrew N. Rebori Designed in the 1920s." *Chicago Tribune*, June 20, 1966.

Hedrich-Blessing Archive. Chicago: Chicago History Museum.

Hitchcock, Henry-Russell and Philip Johnson. *The International Style*. New York: W. W. Norton, 1932.

"House in Ladue, Missouri." *Architectural Forum*, December 1942, 44–48.

"Indoor-Outdoor Living Room." *Architectural Forum*, December 1944, 100–107.

"Isaac Delgado's Museum of Art." *Daily Picayune*, February 12, 1911.

Julius Shulman Photography Archive. Los Angeles: The Getty Research Institute.

Krebs, Albin. "Raymond Loewy, Streamliner of Cars, Planes and Pens, Dies." *The New York Times*, July 15, 1986.

Kuh, Katherine. *My Love Affair with Modern Art*. New York: Arcade Publishing, 2006.

Lackritz Gray, Mary. *A Guide to Chicago's Murals*. Chicago: The University of Chicago Press, 2001.

Lipman, Jean, et al., eds. *The Collector in America*. New York: The Viking Press, 1971.

"Living with the Great." *Vogue*, October 1952, 118–121.

Loring, Kathryn. "Modern Art at Home in a Chicago Apartment." *Chicago Daily Tribune*, August 22, 1954.

Lowe, David Garrard. *Chicago Interiors*. Chicago: Chicago Contemporary Books, 1979.

———. *Lost Chicago*. New York: American Legacy Press, 1985.

"Marxes' Modern." *Life*, October 27, 1952, 92–93.

McGuire, John M. "The Forsyth Saga: Famous Closes Its Legendary Clayton Store." *St. Louis Post-Dispatch Magazine*, June 30, 1991.

"Meet Samuel Marx." *House Beautiful*, November 1945, 120.

Moffett, India. "New Quarters of Arts Club Are Charming." *Chicago Daily Tribune*, December 10, 1936, 21.

Moore, Judy. "Edgar Miller's Reputation Built on Paintings, Stained Glass Work." *Chicago Sun-Times*, July 26, 1985.

Nelson, George and Henry Wright. *Tomorrow's House*. New York: Simon & Schuster, 1945.

"Newly Elected Fellows Citation." *Journal of the American Institute of Architects*, July 1946, 18–21.

"Old Chicago Station Gets New Restaurant." *Architectural Record*, July 1940, 41–43.

O'Neill, Tim. "Shopping in the Suburbs." *St. Louis Post-Dispatch*, January 13, 2004.

"Open Up Interiors for Space, Light, and Air." *House & Home*, October 1954, 146–147.

Othman, Frederick C. "Art Is a Tough Racket, Pal." *Saturday Evening Post*, July 1, 1944, 26–27, 41–42.

Owens, Mitchell. "Remembering Samuel Marx." *Elle Décor*, October/November 1992, 144–149.

Paintings and Drawings: From the Gladys Lloyd Robinson Collection. New York: Parke-Bernet Galleries, 1960.

Parsons, Lee A. *Pre-Columbian Art: The Morton D. May and the Saint Louis Art Museum Collections*. New York: Harper & Row, 1980.

"Patron Wills Art Institute Half-Million: Former Chicagoan Was Trustee." *Chicago Tribune*, January 29, 1964.

Pennoyer, Peter and Anne Walker. *The Architecture of Delano and Aldrich*. New York: W. W. Norton, 2003.

"Pierre Grill: One of New York's Sleeker Hotels Livens Up a Lunchroom." *Architectural Forum*, March 1948, 90–93.

"Private Gallery in Beverly Hills, California." *Architectural Forum*, June 1944, 110–112.

"Profile of a House." *House and Garden*, January 1945, 50–53.

"Reception Lobby Awes Factory Visitors with Splendor and Elegance." *Architectural Forum*, September 1949, 92–93.

Richardson, John. *The Sorcerer's Apprentice: Picasso, Provence and Douglas Cooper*. New York: Knopf, 2001.

Robinson, Edward G. *All My Yesterdays*. New York: Hawthorn Books, 1973.

Robinson, Jane. *Edward G. Robinson's World of Art*. New York: Harper & Row, 1971.

Ross, David E. "Department Stores." *David Ross, one of the last living liberals*, 2005. http://www.rossde.com/editorials/edtl_deptstores.html.

Russell, John. *Matisse: Father & Son*. New York: Harry N. Abrams, 1999.

Salny, Stephen M. *The Country Houses of David Adler*. New York: W. W. Norton & Company, 2001.

———. *Frances Elkins: Interior Design*. New York: W. W. Norton, 2005.

"Samuel A. Marx Rites Sunday at Natchez, Miss." *Chicago Sun-Times*, January 19, 1964.

"Samuel Marx Services Today at Graveside." *Natchez Democrat*, January 19, 1964.

"Samuel Marx, Top Architect, Dies at Age 78: Was Art Collector and Artist." *Chicago Tribune*, January 18, 1964.

Schulze, Franz. *Mies Van Der Rohe: A Critical Biography*. Chicago: The University of Chicago Press, 1985.

"Setting for a Fine Picture Collection: The Hubbard Woods Home of Mr. Max Epstein." *Country Life*, January 1936, 50–53.

"Snapshots: Samuel A. Marx." *Interiors*, September 1941, 41–43.

The Arts Club of Chicago: The Collection 1916–1996. Chicago: Congress Printing Company, 1997.

The Arts Club of Chicago: Seventy-Fifth Anniversary. Chicago: Rohner Printing Company, 1992.

"The New House 194X." *Architectural Forum*, September 1942, 130–131.

"The Pump Room." *Architectural Forum*, July 1940, 21–24.

"The Pump Room, Hotel Ambassador, Chicago." *Architectural Record*, August 1943, 73–74.

"The Year's Work: These Five Interiors for Work, for Living, and for Play, Have Been Completed by Leading Designers and Architects." *Interiors*, August 1942, 29–54.

Thorne, Martha, ed. *David Adler, Architect: The Elements of Style*. New Haven: Yale University Press in association with The Art Institute of Chicago, 2002.

"Traditional Modern." *House & Garden*, January 1941, 40.

Trowbridge Archive. Chicago: Chicago History Museum.

van Roessel, Annemarie. "Ernest Alton Grunsfeld, III." Chicago Architects Oral History Project, Art Institute of Chicago, January 15–24, 2004, http://www.artic.edu/aic/libraries/caohp/grunsfeld.html.

Vogel, Carol. "32 Works of Art by Masters Left to Met and the Modern." *New York Times*, November 25, 1996.

Watson, Forbes (foreword). *John Quinn 1970–1925: Collection of Paintings, Water Colors, Drawings and Sculpture*. Huntington, NY: Pidgeon Hill Press, 1926.

Weigle, Edith. "They Live Amid Art." *Chicago Daily Tribune*, May 25, 1958.

Whitaker, Jan. *Service and Style: How the American Department Store Fashioned the Middle Class*. New York: St. Martin's Press, 2006.

Who's Who in Chicago and Vicinity. Chicago: The A. N. Marquis Company, 1926.

Who's Who in Chicago and Vicinity. Chicago: The A. N. Marquis Company, 1941.

Zimmer, Jim L. *John Warner Norton*. Illinois: Illinois State Museum, 1993.

CHRONOLOGY

1885 *August 27: Born in Natchez, Mississippi, son of Annie Baszinsky and Jonas Marx.*

1903 *Graduates Phillips Exeter Academy in New Hampshire.*

1907 *Graduates Massachusetts Institute of Technology with a Bachelor of Science in Architecture.*

1907–09 *Continues architectural training at the Ecole des Beaux-Arts in Paris, in the Ateliers Chifflot and Duquesne.*

1910 *Moves to Chicago and works briefly as a draftsman for the firm of Shepley, Rutan and Coolidge. Enters and wins national competition to design the Isaac Delgado Museum of Art in New Orleans, Louisiana. Forms firm of Lebenbaum and Marx with partner Fred Lebenbaum.*

1911 *December: Isaac Delgado Museum of Art opens.*

1912 *Lebenbaum and Marx design country residence for advertising pioneer Albert D. Lasker at Pomander Walk in Glencoe, Illinois.*

1915 *June 10: Marries Margaret Schaffner, daughter of Joseph Schaffner, partner in men's clothier Hart, Schaffner and Marx.*

1916 *Fred Lebenbaum dies. Continues to practice on his own as Samuel A. Marx, Architect.*

1928 *Hired by investment firm A.G. Becker to design Chicago offices and commissions a site-specific mural by French artist Bernard Boutet de Monvel. Designs interiors for two New York City residences, one for Arthur Lehman and one for Mrs. Walter Hirsch.*

1930 *Designs Edgecliff, the country estate of industrialist Max Epstein in the Hubbard Woods section of Winnetka, Illinois. Having divorced Margaret sometime in the late 1920s, marries artist Lora Flanagan in the early '30s. Lora had studied sculpture with Carl Milles at the Cranbrook Academy in Bloomfield Hills, Michigan.*

1933 *Designs first aluminum train car for the Pullman Company, which makes its debut at the 1933 Century-of-Progress Exposition in Chicago. Hired by Edward Sonnenschein to design a room to display his collection of fine Chinese jades at his house in Glencoe. Noel L. Flint becomes an associate architect at Marx's firm.*

1934 *Remodels Glencoe residence of Henry R. Levy, originally designed by Howard van Doren Shaw for Moses Born. Shortly thereafter also remodels the house of Born's daughter, Florence, and her husband, Harold E. Foreman, located on the family's lakeside property.*

1936 *Renovates Robert F. Bensinger house in Glencoe, also originally designed by Shaw. November: Divorces Lora Marx.*

1937 *Designs neo-baroque dining room for new location of the Arts Club of Chicago in the South Tower of the Wrigley Building at 410 North Michigan Avenue. Designs apartment for Mortimer B. Harris at 1540 North Lake Shore Drive. April 4: Marries Florene May Straus at the Beverly Hills home of her brother Wilbur May.*

1938 *October: The Pump Room at the Ambassador East Hotel in Chicago's Gold Coast opens to wide acclaim.*

1939 *Completes the design of his apartment at 1325 North Astor Street, just blocks away from the Pump Room. Attends the Golden Gate Exposition in San Francisco with Florene; they purchase furniture, objects, and carpets for their new home as well as Georges Braque's* Yellow Tablecloth *of 1935, the start of their distinguished collection of modern art.*

1940 *Adds several important works to art collection including Henri Matisse's* Apples *and* Variations on a Still Life After de Heem, *which he purchases through New York art dealer Pierre Matisse.*

1941 *The May Company opens its flagship store, designed by Marx with associate architect Albert C. Martin, on Wilshire Boulevard in Los Angeles. Completes a modern house in Ladue, Missouri, for Morton D. May. Remodels the lounge and dining rooms of the Tavern Club in Chicago. Designs the Cotillion Room and the Rotunda in New York's Hotel Pierre. Visits famed actor and art collector Edward G. Robinson and is hired to remodel his Tudor-style house on North Rexford Drive.*

1942 *Acquires Constantin Brancusi's white marble sculpture* Bird in Space *of 1923, the first version of the artist's famous subject; it is now at the Metropolitan Museum of Art in New York.*

1943 *Designs Chicago apartment for Mary and Leigh B. Block at 1260 North Astor Street.*

1944 *Completes Robinson house and private art gallery. Opening of Pierre Grill at Hotel Pierre in New York with artwork by Edgar Miller and modern kitchen visible from dining room.*

1946 *Awarded the American Institute of Architect's Award for Excellence.*

1947 *Begins two-year design of apartment for Joseph L. Block at 1325 North Astor Street. Designs Chicago apartment and offices for Arthur Keating, head of Ekco Cookware. Designs interiors of townhouse at 1328 North State Street for Lillian Florsheim.*

1948 *Designs Bel Air residence of Kitty and Mervyn LeRoy. Opening of May Company department store on Crenshaw Boulevard in Los Angeles and the Clayton location of the Famous Barr stores, both designed by Marx. Adds Matisse's* Goldfish *of 1915–1916 to his collection.*

1950 *Purchases Joan Miró's 1917* Portrait of E. C. Ricart *from Pierre Matisse.*

1952 *Designs the Alexander Hamilton Memorial in Chicago's Lincoln Park. Purchases Henri Matisse's* The Moroccans *directly from the artist with the help of Alfred H. Barr, Jr., with the provision that the painting will later be donated to the Museum of Modern Art in New York. Joins the Board of Trustees at the Art Institute of Chicago.*

1953 *Florene May elected to the Board of Trustees at the Museum of Modern Art in New York.*

1954 *Designs Holmby Hills residence of Florene's brother Tom May and his wife Anita. William Haines, Hollywood decorator and longtime friend, designs the interiors in a successful collaboration between architect and designer.*

1955 *Designs residence for Dr. and Mrs. Irving Stein in Glencoe, Illinois. Completes other modern country houses around the same time for clients such as P. D. Block, Jr., and Kurt Friend. Commissioned by Lester Kaufman to design modern house in Aurora, Illinois.*

1956 *Completes apartment for Ruth and Harvey Kaplan at 1325 North Astor Street.*

1957 *Designs suspended Birdcage Bar in the Rotunda of the Hotel Pierre, and takes on design of the Pierre Marques Hotel in Acapulco, Mexico, for J. Paul Getty on property adjacent to the billionaire oilman's own secluded retreat.*

1958 *Alfred H. Barr, Jr. facilitates Marx's purchase of Matisse's* Woman on a High Stool *from the artist's estate.*

1960 *Marxes attend Picasso retrospective at the Tate Gallery in London.*

1962 *Marxes sell their Glencoe and Chicago homes and move to New York City where Florene's daughter Nancy lives with her family. Establish residency at the Hotel Westbury on Madison Avenue.*

1964 *January 17: Dies in New York City at the age of seventy-eight; buried in Natchez, Mississippi.*

1965 *November:* The School of Paris *exhibition of the Marx collection opens at the Museum of Modern Art and travels to museums around the country and to Mexico.*

CREDITS

Every effort has been made to locate holders of copyright; any omissions will be corrected in future printings.

From the Stanley D. Anderson Architectural Archives: 211 (top).

Drapery made from a Liebes textile, 1939. Image is courtesy of the Dorothy Liebes papers, 1925–1973, in the Archives of American Art, Smithsonian Institution: 211 (bottom).

Courtesy *L'architecture d'aujourd'hui*; nos. 5–6, June 1937: 21.

© 2007 Artists Rights Society (ARS), New York / ADAGP, Paris: 115, 116, 117, 192, 194–195,198, 200 (top), 200 (bottom).

© 2007 Artists Rights Society (ARS), New York / SIAE, Rome: 131.

© 2007 Artists Rights Society (ARS), New York / VG Bild-Kunst, Bonn: 197.

Courtesy of The Art Institute of Chicago, Archives: 28.

New Orleans Museum of Art, New Orleans, LA, c.1915–1920. Exterior view. Historic Architecture and Landscape Image Collection, Ryerson and Burnham Archives, The Art Institute of Chicago. Reproduction © The Art Institute of Chicago: 22 (inset).

Samuel A. Marx, American. 1885–1964, *End Table*, 1944, pine and glass, height: 25 1/4 in., width:17 15/16 in., Gift of Mr. Leigh B. Block, 1981.174, The Art Institute of Chicago. Photography © The Art Institute of Chicago: 193 (bottom).

Sam Marx Residence, n.d Interior view. Institutional Archives, The Art Institute of Chicago. Reproduction © The Art Institute of Chicago: 120–121, 126, 129, 131.

Max Epstein Residence, Winnetka, IL, c.1931–1936. Interior view. Historic Architecture and Landscape Image Collection, Ryerson and Burnham Archives, The Art Institute of Chicago. Reproduction © The Art Institute of Chicago: 62.

Chicago History Museum: HB-07051F, photo by Hedrich-Blessing, Back Jacket; ICHi-50351 Trowbridge, 24 (inset); ICHi-19834, Photographer unknown, 24–25; HB-07198, photo by Hedrich-Blessing, 27; ICHi-50251, Trowbridge, 30; ICHi-50352, Photographer unknown, 31; HB-11899M, photo by Hedrich-Blessing, 34 (top); HB-11899E, photo by Hedrich-Blessing, 34 (bottom); HB-11899C, photo by Hedrich-Blessing, 35; HB-15293C, photo by Hedrich-Blessing, 36; HB-15293G, photo by Hedrich-Blessing, 37; ICHi-36664b, Photographer unknown, 38–39; ICHi-50214, Trowbridge, 50–51; ICHi-50217, Trowbridge, 52; ICHi-50218, Trowbridge, 53 (top); ICHi-50213, Trowbridge, 53 (bottom); ICHi-50216, Trowbridge, 54–55; HB-07662, photo by Hedrich-Blessing, 83; HB-05666C, photo by Hedrich-Blessing, 85; HB-06910C, photo by Hedrich-Blessing, 86 (top); HB-06910A, photo by Hedrich-Blessing, 86 (bottom); HB-06910B, photo by Hedrich- Blessing, 87; HB-05688A, photo by Hedrich-Blessing, 88–89; HB04408, photo by Hedrich-Blessing, 90; HB-04408A, photo by Hedrich-Blessing, 91; HB-06251D, photo by Hedrich-Blessing, 92; HB-06251A, photo by Hedrich-Blessing, 93; HB-05824D, photo by Hedrich-Blessing, 94; HB-05824E, photo by Hedrich-Blessing, 95; HB-5824B, photo by Hedrich-Blessing, 96–97; HB-15182, photo by Hedrich-Blessing, 106–107; HB-22015A, photo by Hedrich-Blessing, 108 (top); HB-22015H, photo by Hedrich-Blessing, 108 (bottom); HB-22015C, photo by Hedrich-Blessing, 109; HB-22015O, photo by Hedrich-Blessing, 111; ICHi-50455, Photographer Unknown, 112–113; HB-06194C, photo by Hedrich-Blessing, 114 (top right); HB-06194-B, photo by Hedrich-Blessing, 114 (top left); HB-06194S, photo by Hedrich-Blessing, 119; HB-06194O, photo by Hedrich-Blessing, 125 (top); HB-06194Z, photo by Hedrich-Blessing, 125 (bottom); HB-06194W, photo by Hedrich-Blessing, 132; HB-06194Y, photo by Hedrich-Blessing, 133 (top left); HB-06194X, photo by Hedrich-Blessing, 133 (top right); HB-06194Q, photo by Hedrich-Blessing, 133 (bottom left); HB-06194P, photo by Hedrich-Blessing, 133 (bottom right); HB-07051W, photo by Hedrich-Blessing, 136–137; HB-07051B, photo by Hedrich-Blessing, 138; HB-07051V, photo by Hedrich-Blessing, 139; HB-07051G, photo by Hedrich-Blessing, 140; HB-07051F, photo by Hedrich-Blessing, 141; HB-07051J, photo by Hedrich-Blessing, 143; HB-09068B, photo by Hedrich-Blessing, 149 (top); HB-07850C, photo by Hedrich-Blessing, 168; HB-07850B, photo by Hedrich-Blessing, 169.

Hedrich-Blessing / Copyright © 1941 Condé Nast Publications Inc.: 116.

Herbert Matter / Copyright © 1952 Condé Nast Publications Inc.: 193 (top).

Courtesy of *House and Garden* / Condé Nast Publications Inc.: 73, 74.

François Dischinger: Author photograph, back flap.

Getty Images / Time & Life Pictures / Photograph by John Bryson: 165.

Getty Images / Time & Life Pictures / Photograph by Herbert Gehr: 82.

Getty Images / Time & Life Pictures / Photograph by Charles E. Steinheimer: 210.

Photograph by William Grigsby. Reproduced from "Collectors: Mary and Leigh Block," by Francine du Plessix, *Art in America*, September–October 1966. Brant Publications, Inc: 190, 200 (center and bottom).

Photograph by William Grigsby. Reproduced from "The Flawless Eye: Mary and Leigh Block," *The Collector in America*, by Jean Lipman and the Editors of Art in America. Courtesy Brant Publications, Inc.: 191, 192, 196–197, 198–199, 200 (top).

Photographs by Bob Hiemstra: 120, 123, 188, 201, 214, 215.

The Historic New Orleans Collection, accession no.1979.325.5807: 22–23.

Courtesy of *House Beautiful*: 195.

© J. Paul Getty Trust. Used with permission. Julius Shulman Photography Archive Research Library at the Getty Research Institute: 144–145, 148, 149 (bottom), 150–151, 170–172, 173 (top), 175, 177–185.

Chris Kennedy DESIGNbase® Northhampton, MA: 116.

Library of Congress, Geography and Map Division: 9.

Liz O'Brien Gallery: Cover, 2, 6–7, 130, 173 (bottom), 174, 176, 204 (top).

Mary Harris Marks: 64, 66 (top), 67 (top), 69 (left), 70.

© 2007 Succession H. Matisse, Paris / Artists Rights Society (ARS), New York: 124, 125 (bottom), 128, 129, 192.

Terry McKay: 13, 56–61, 63.

Courtesy of Mississippi Department of Archives and History: 9 (inset right).

Missouri Historical Society, St Louis. Copy after Erwin Carl Schmidt: 152 (top).

Missouri Historical Society, St Louis. Schapiro, Ted: 153.

Missouri Historical Society, St Louis. Dorrill Studio: 152 (bottom).

MIT Museum: Jacket, cover, 14, 16–17, 18–19.

Digital Image © The Museum of Modern Art / Licensed by SCALA / Art Resource, NY: 117, 118, 124, 128.

Arnold Newman / Getty Images: 115, 122–123, 188–189, 194.

Collection of The New-York Historical Society: 40–43, 98–103.

Art & Architecture Collection, Miriam and Ira D. Wallach Division of Art, Prints and Photographs, The New York Public Library, Astor, Lenox and Tilden Foundations: 44–49, 78–79, 80–81, 84, 104–105, 142.

Styling by Rebecca Omweg: 1, 5, 65, 66 (bottom both), 69 (left), 71, 76–77.

Photography by Maynard Parker. Courtesy of the Huntington Library, San Marino, California: 154–161, 164, 166–167.

Academy Archives. Class of 1945 Library. Phillips Exeter Academy: Jacket flap.

© 2007 Estate of Pablo Picasso / Artists Rights Society (ARS), New York: 5, 118, 119, 190, 197, 198, 200 (top).

Private Collection: 32–33.

Roger-Viollet: 20, 21 (inset).

Susan B. Rubnitz: 202–203, 204 (bottom), 205, 206–207, 209.

Collection of Sherlee Rhine, interior design by Steven Volpe, photography by Patrik Argast: 67 (bottom).

Patricia May Staab: 8, 9 (insets left and center), 10–12, 15.

Residence of Dr. Milton Vainder: Front jacket, 4, 72, 75–77.

Wright and Brian Franczyk Photography: 127, 208.

Photographs by Björn Wallander: Front jacket, endpapers, 1, 3–5, 65, 66 (bottom both), 68, 69 (left), 71, 72, 75–77, 204 (bottom), 205–207, 209.

INDEX

ABOVE Modern chinoiserie chair, circa 1940.

I N D E X

ABOVE Dining chair with Dorothy Liebes fabric, circa 1950.

In memory of my parents, Marie Ayers and John J. O'Brien, whose sense of joy has been a beautiful and lasting gift to me and to everyone who knew them.

Any book project calls for the contributions of many people and I am indebted to all my family, friends, and colleagues who gave so generously of their time and support.

Over the past year I have been reminded continually of my good fortune in having so many wonderful people in my life, and I am grateful to have this opportunity to express my heartfelt thanks.

First, I thank Gary Cohen, who has urged me to do this book since we first met more than ten years ago. He has been there for me every step of the way, and this book would not have been possible without his unwavering support, guidance, and help with research, reading, and editing.

To everyone who works with me at the gallery, I thank you for your hard work, commitment, and camaraderie. To Doria Kalt, who manages to keep things running smoothly through thick and thin, and has also proved to be a research and book-finding whiz, thank you and bravo for a job well done. Also thanks to Lizbeth Cebellos, Cassandra Morgan, Margaret Smith, and Megan Strecker who contribute so much every day and make going to work a pleasure.

To the team at the Pointed Leaf Press I owe a world of gratitude. First, a warm thank-you to publisher Suzanne Slesin whose intelligence, courage, and commitment to making the best possible book were a constant source of inspiration. Thank you also to art director Stafford Cliff—his brilliant and insightful design holds the book together and brings Marx and his work to life. I can hardly imagine reaching the finish line without the organization, dedication, positive input, and cheering-on of managing editor Jane Creech—thank you, Jane! Thanks to Rebecca Omweg and Björn Wallander whose beautiful color photographs add so much to the finished product. Many thanks also to Terra Chalberg, Christine Owen, Dominick Santise, Jr., Dan Shaw, and Anne Hellman White. I am in awe of your hard work, talent, and creativity.

Many people connected to Samuel Marx made their time, photo albums, letters, homes, and memories available. I am deeply grateful to all of them. Thank you to Patricia May Staab, who helped with biographical data, personal reminiscences, and family photographs; her discovery of the early Natchez photos was nothing short of a Rosebud moment! Countless others have helped with background, introductions, research, and encouragement. They include: Marilynn Alsdorf, Joan Arenberg, Claire Holland Barancik, Susan and Wayne Benjamin, Paul Bergmann, Avis Berman, Stuart Cohen, Henry Czapla, Mr. and Mrs. John Daimel, Terri and Alfred D'Ancona, Mr. and Mrs. Stanley Freehling, Harold Foreman, Jr., Ernest A. Grunsfeld III, Leslie and David Helfand, Linda LeRoy Janklow, Alan and Charlotte Kaplan, Elizabeth and Thomas Keim, Mark Mamolen, Mary Harris Marks, Kay Mayer, Terry McKay, Rabbi Yocheved Mintz and Dr. Alan Mintz, Susan B. Rubnitz, Tim Samuelson, Franz Schulze, Mrs. George Sidney, Ginger Sonnenschein, Henry Stern, Mr. and Mrs. Tom Steward, Daniel Swett, Dr. Milton Vainder, Alvin Whitehead, Ruth Louise Young, and Larry Zagoda.

Dozens of archivists and librarians have contributed their considerable skills and enthusiasm to the task of pulling together and gaining access to the documents related to Marx's life and career. My grateful appreciation to everyone at the Chicago History Museum, especially Olivia Mahoney, Lesley Martin, Rob Medina, and Erin Tikovitsch for their help with the Hedrich-Blessing photo archive and general Chicago history. Thanks also to the staff at the Art Institute of Chicago for their thorough research and impressive detective work, especially Lori Boyer, Barbara Hinde, Denise Mahony, Aimee L. Marshall, Nathaniel Parks, Eleanor Pearlstein, Bart Ryckbosch, and Mary Woolever. Thanks to Kathy Cattong at the Arts Club of Chicago. A warm thank you to Arthur Miller and Sara Woodbury at the Lake Forest College Library, who were there from square one. Many thanks to my friends at the Cooper-Hewitt Design Library, Elizabeth Broman, Jennifer Coleman, and Stephen Van Dyk, for their help with reference materials and periodicals. Laura Knott at the MIT Museum provided prompt and detailed responses to all my questions. Thanks to Shelly C. Bronk, Edouard L. Desroches, and Thomas A. Wharton at Phillips Exeter Academy. I am indebted to several people at the Smithsonian Archives of American Art, including Wendy Hurlock Baker, Elizabeth Botten, and Catherine S. Gaines for their assistance with the Dorothy Liebes papers, and also to Joy Weiner for her considerable research skills. Thanks to Sheila Cork, John Keefe, and Lisa Rotondo-McCord at the New Orleans Museum of Art; to John Magill at the New Orleans Historical Society; to Barbara Haigh and Teri Tillman with the Natchez Historical Society.

On the North Shore I thank Tina Herman of the Lake Shore Country Club, Ellen Shubart at the Glencoe Historical Society; Peter Scalera at the Glencoe Historic Preservation Committee, Richard Stumpf at the Park District of Highland Park, and Paul Bergmann at the Stanley D. Anderson Architectural Archives. Thanks to Dr. Alice L. Birney at the Library of Congress; Catherine Burke and Matt Cook at the Illinois Institute of Technology; Erin Chase at the Huntington Library in San Marino, California; Anne Blecksmith and Julio Sims at the Getty Research Center; Ned Comstock at the University of Southern California Cinema-Television Library; and Anne Fordyce and David Keegan at the Lasker Foundation. Many thanks to Michelle Elliott, Thomas Grischkowsky, Milan Hughston, and Kathleen Tunney at the Museum of Modern Art in New York; thanks to Richard Parks, Inge DuPont, Sylvie Merian, and Vanessa Pintado at the Morgan Library Reading Room for their gracious help with the Pierre Matisse Gallery papers.

I consider it a great blessing that I love my job, which is largely because of all the talented and passionate people I interact with on a regular basis. Colleagues and friends have provided help with research, insights, and encouragement and I extend to them my heartfelt gratitude and admiration. Thank you to: Jeffrey Bilhuber, R. Louis Bofferding, Norman Brosterman, Ralph and Steven Chait of the R. M. Chait Galleries, Inc.; Sally Forbes and David Garrard Lowe of the Beaux Arts Alliance; Michael Formica, Jessica R. Friedman, Brian Gracie, Jacques Grange, William Hall, Bob Hiemstra, Jane Holzer, Michel Hurst, Chris Kennedy, Valerie Komor, Delphine and Reed Krakoff, Oscar Mandes, Peter Margonelli, Anne-Claire Marsaud, Shawn Marsh, Richard Norton, Pierre Passebon and Nathalie Peters of the Galerie du Passage; Bruce Pelletier; James Potsch of Wright in Chicago; Roger Prigent; Andrew Raimist, Sherlee Rhine; and Sally Rosen, Alan Rosenberg, David Roth, Steven Salny, Jeffrey Schaper, Jean Smith, Jason Stein, Robert Swope, and Steven Volpe. Very special thanks to Julie Thoma Wright, Richard Wright and everyone at Wright who has contributed so graciously to making this book possible.

Finally, I thank Peter Yeakel whose steadfast love has made all the difference in my life. You are my rock, my anchor, and my home.

Liz O'Brien
May 2007

Pointed Leaf Press would like to thank Debra Castellano, Cynthia Crippen, Jennifer Dixon, Claire Fortune, David Friedlander, Gita Gidwani, Leigh Montville, Claude Picasso, Jon Scott, Michael Steinberg, Sylvie Vautier, Selma Weiner, Glenn Gerish and Kelly Sipos at Quebecor World Premedia, and Hung Chu, Vince Hamilton and Kosuke Saeki at Toppan.

Front jacket and page 4: Samuel Marx updated the dining room of the Robert F. Bensinger house in 1936 with a black marble fireplace and circular niche to showcase sculpture.

Back jacket: The helical staircase at the Morton D. May house in Ladue, Missouri, was sculpted in the round like a twisting ribbon in the shape of a giant conch shell.

Cover: Strong, sculptural andirons of interlocking rectangles of brushed nickel were made for the Alfred Koolish residence in Bel Air, California.

Endpapers: Executed in the late 1930s, this chest of drawers was designed for the dining room of a private residence in Chicago. The notched, zigzag form of the face and the refined lacquer finish attest to the virtuoso skills of the William J. Quigley, Inc. workrooms.

Half title left: A detail of hand-plastered walls from a Chicago residence illustrates the subtly luxurious finishes that made Marx's interiors so distinctive.

Half title right: A two-door cabinet raised on a rectangular plinth and with a block handle, dates from the early forties. William J. Quigley, the Chicago cabinetmaker, executed the design and finished it in the ivory-colored crackle lacquer that became a signature of Marx's work.

Page 2: A secretary bookcase, circa 1940, in crackle lacquer, with shelves lined in silver leaf, incorporates many design elements of Marx's architectural work. The stylized Palladian features of the large circular glass opening and the recessed arch at the base, anticipate the postmodern designs of the 1980s.

Title page: Marx used fossil stone extensively in both private residences and public spaces. Its richly textured surface softened the bold geometric forms of the architect's wall treatments and fireplaces.

Page 5: In a Chicago apartment, a ceramic plate by Pablo Picasso rests on an unusual fireplace surround dating from 1937. Made of fossil stone with a faux-painted overmantel, it is a quintessential Marx touch.

Contents: A chest of drawers, circa 1950, with clapboard-style front in quarter-sawn oak is distinguished by its unusual limed finish rubbed with touches of black stain and aluminum powder.

First edition

10 9 8 7 6 5 4 3 2 1

Library of Congress Control Number: 2007928208

ISBN-10: 0-9777875-2-4
ISBN-13: 978-0-9777875-2-4